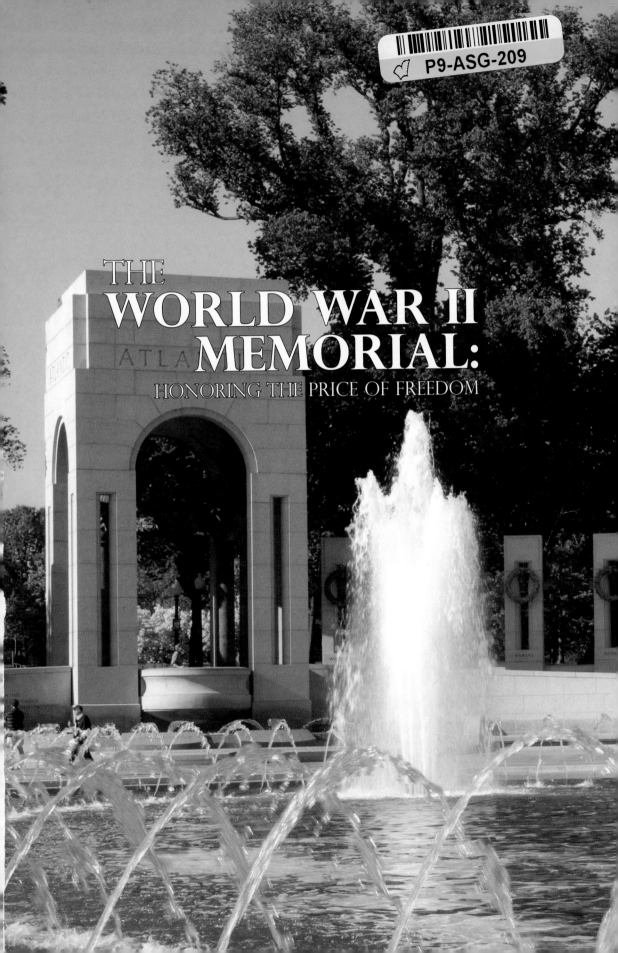

THE
WORLD WAR II
MEMORIAL:

HONORING THE PRICE OF FREEDOM

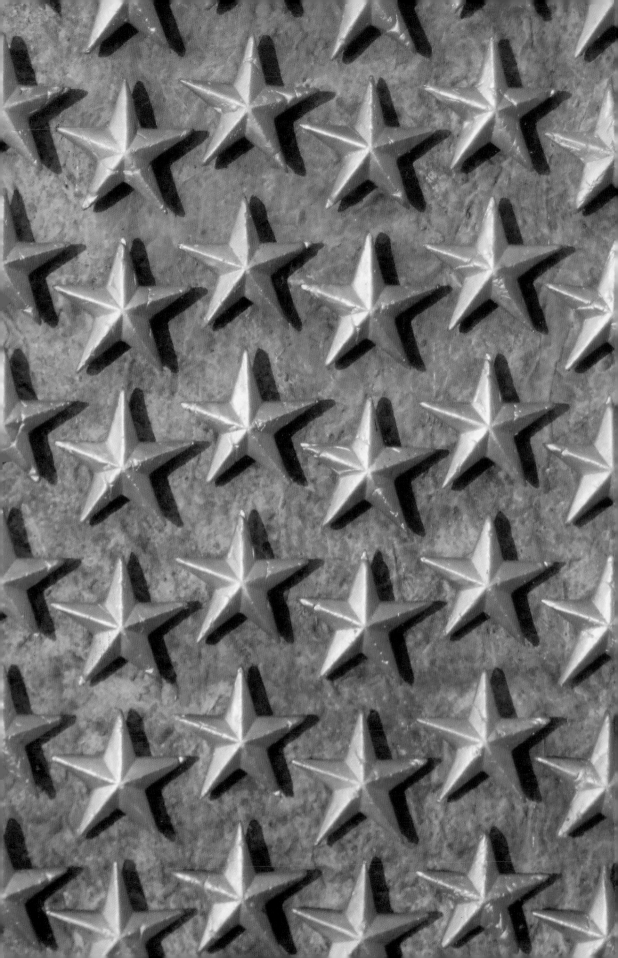

THE
WORLD WAR II
MEMORIAL:
HONORING THE PRICE OF FREEDOM

MICHELLE A. KROWL

Featuring the photography of Carol M. Highsmith

Eastern National
Serving the Visitors to America's
National Parks and Other Public Trusts

Facing the title page: *Field of gold stars on Freedom Wall.* Author's collection

Find Kilroy! Kilroy can be found on the memorial itself, and his legend is discussed elsewhere in this book. Can you find them both?

The Donning Company Publishers
184 Business Park Drive, Suite 206
Virginia Beach, VA 23462

Library of Congress Cataloging-in-Publication Data

Krowl, Michelle A.
  The World War II Memorial : honoring the price of freedom / by Michelle A. Krowl.
     p. cm.
  Includes bibliographical references.
  ISBN-13: 978-1-57864-438-4 (soft cover : alk. paper)
  1. World War II Memorial (Washington, D.C.) 2. World War, 1939-1945--Monuments--Washington (D.C.) 3. War memorials--Washington (D.C.) 4. World War, 1939-1945--United States. I. Title. II. Title: World War Two Memorial. III. Title: World War 2 Memorial.
  D836.W37K76 2007
  940.53'73--dc22
                    2007020467

Printed in the United States of America at Walsworth Publishing Company

CONTENTS

p. 7		*Welcome*
p. 8	**Chapter 1:**	*The World at War: The Second World War*
p. 58	**Chapter 2:**	*Constructing a Memorial*
p. 64	**Chapter 3:**	*The World War II Memorial*
p. 106		*National Park Service Sites of Relevance*
p. 107		*For Further Reading*
p. 108		*Acknowledgments*
p. 110		*Notes*

Twilight time at the Reflecting Pool, where both the Washington Monument and World War II Memorial are echoed in the still water.

State pillars illuminated at night. Photo by Terry Adams/National Park Service

★★★ WELCOME

UNITY. If only one word could be used to describe the American experience in World War II and the symbolism behind the World War II Memorial, it would be "unity." More than any other war in the nation's history, the Second World War required America's military forces to unite for victory in multiple theaters of war fought around the globe, its allies to unite against common enemies, and the home front to unite behind the total war effort. Unlike traditional war memorials dedicated solely to the men who did the fighting, the World War II Memorial celebrates the combined American efforts of the soldiers in the field, the personnel who supported the military, and the civilians on the home front who contributed to achieving ultimate victory. The design elements of the memorial acknowledge not only the soldiers at the Battle of the Bulge and the Marines who slogged through island hopping in the Pacific, but also the women who served as nurses and worked as "Rosie the Riveters" in the vital aircraft industry. The pivotal D-Day invasion of 1944 is highlighted, as is the importance of agricultural production on the home front in keeping the armies fed and in fighting form. The memorial physically unites the Pacific and Atlantic Theaters through the Freedom Wall, which mourns the toll each theater took in terms of human lives. Pillars representing the American states and territories during the war are linked by bronze ropes, tying the nation together in a common bond of victory. The memorial thus can provide visitors with a sense of America's participation in the war itself.

CHAPTER ONE

THE WORLD AT WAR

THE SECOND WORLD WAR

The Second World War was truly a world war in that battles were fought around the globe. For some nations, their part of the war was waged in a specific theater, like the Pacific Ocean or Eastern Europe. For the United States, however, World War II was really two wars: one against Japan in the Pacific, and another against Germany and other Axis powers in the Atlantic Theater. As such, the road to American involvement in the war took two separate paths.

The Gathering Storm Over Europe

On the European, or Atlantic, side, the roots of the Second World War could be traced to unresolved issues from the First World War (1914–1918). Although U.S. President Woodrow Wilson had hoped the bloodshed of World War I would be made meaningful by a peace treaty and a League of Nations that would allow future conflicts to be solved short of war, his British, French, and Italian counterparts also sought to punish the Germans. The resulting Treaty of Versailles (1919) forced Germany to accept responsibility for the war, to demilitarize, and to monetarily reimburse the victorious Allies for their losses. The League of Nations ultimately proved ineffective, however, especially after political disputes at home kept the United States from joining it.

The devastation of World War I lingered in many ways. Many European countries became economically unstable because of war debts, while the defeated nations also forfeited territories that had formed part of their colonial empires. Political revolutions threatened to topple governments in places like Italy, and socialist political movements attracted increasing support elsewhere in Europe. In Germany, the Treaty of Versailles remained unpopular, as did reparation payments. In addition, postwar disillusionment arose in many nations when it appeared that the terrible cost in human life had not brought about any significant changes. The situation in Europe became even grimmer after the American stock market crashed in October 1929, plunging the U.S. economy into a prolonged depression and dragging European markets down with it.

Several individuals exploited this atmosphere of economic and cultural uncertainty to gain power for themselves. Fascist leader Benito Mussolini took control of Italy in 1922. While Italians marveled that under his regime the trains finally ran on time, Mussolini and his black-shirted army ruled with a heavy hand. In Germany, Adolf Hitler was appointed chancellor in 1933, and once his National Socialist, or Nazi, party took the reins of power, he began building his "Third Reich." In Spain, years of political turmoil led to the Spanish Civil War (1936–1939), in which the Nationalist army under Francisco Franco triumphed over the Republican opposition.

Axis allies Benito Mussolini (left) and Adolf Hitler enjoy a procession in Munich, Germany, in June 1940. The smiles would fade as both leaders watched their dreams of empire shatter during the war. National Archives, 242-EB-7-38

Row upon row of German soldiers assembled for a mass roll call at Nuremberg, Germany, in November 1935. The impressive showing demonstrated that Hitler's nationalistic program and propaganda attracted a huge following and served as an illustration to the outside world of Nazi strength and domination. National Archives, 200-GR-12

Throughout the 1930s, Hitler attracted disillusioned Germans by refusing to accept the terms of the Versailles treaty, appealed to German nationalism, and promised to restore territory stripped from Germany at the end of World War I. Explaining that Germany needed more *lebensraum* (living space), Hitler took over the Sudetenland, Rhineland, and Austria. At the same time, Hitler violated the terms of the Versailles treaty by enlarging Germany's military and establishing an air force, called the *Luftwaffe*.

No one seemed prepared to stop Hitler. He signed a pact with Mussolini in 1936, and at Munich in 1938, Britain and France appeased Hitler, providing he agreed not to take any more territory. Although British Prime Minister Neville Chamberlain announced that the Munich agreement would lead to "peace in our time," Hitler had no intention of fulfilling his promises and instead took over Czechoslovakia in 1939. Nazi Germany and Josef Stalin's communist Soviet Union (USSR) shocked the world in August 1939 by announcing they had signed a non-aggression pact. Then, on September 1, 1939, Hitler invaded Poland, which fell in a little over a month. Britain and France declared war on Germany on September 3, 1939, and World War II had officially begun.

For the first year of the war, things went badly for the Allies, led by Britain and France. Not having to worry about the Soviets to the east, Hitler in 1940 was able to unleash a *blitzkrieg* (lightning war) to the west, using a combination of planes, tanks, and infantry to overwhelm his opponents. In quick succession, the Germans conquered Denmark, Norway, the Netherlands, Belgium, and France by June 1940. Italy entered the war on Germany's side in June. In addition to the land war, German U-boats (*unterseeboot*, or submarine) patrolled the Atlantic Ocean hoping to interrupt trade to Britain, beginning a prolonged battle for control of the Atlantic.

German troops parade through Warsaw, Poland, September 1939. National Archives, 200-SFF-52

During the Battle of Britain, the British relied on radar and a system of spotters to alert authorities about incoming German planes. This spotter is stationed on a rooftop not far from St. Paul's Cathedral. National Archives, 306-NT-901B-3

The British withdrew their forces from Dunkirk, Belgium, at the end of May and prepared themselves for the inevitable German offensive against Britain, which came in July 1940. The Luftwaffe bombed British airfields, radar towers, factories, and eventually London itself. The Royal Air Force (RAF) stretched itself to the limits to fight the Luftwaffe in the air, while civilians steeled themselves for *blitz* bombings on the ground. By mid-September, the RAF and English fortitude convinced Hitler to call off plans for an invasion of England. Even though the bombings continued for months, the British had won the Battle of Britain and, perhaps as importantly, won the sympathy of the American public.

Hitler made a colossal blunder in June 1941 by violating his treaty with Stalin and invading the Soviet Union. Despite early successes, Hitler underestimated Russian resolve to resist invasion and the amount of time it would take to achieve his objectives. His drive into the Soviet Union stalled, his armies faced hardships in the Russian winter, and by attacking the Soviets, Hitler made Stalin a potential ally for the British.

In the United States, President Franklin D. Roosevelt (FDR) anxiously watched developments in Europe but could do little to help the Allies. Americans too had been disillusioned by the carnage of World War I and took steps to isolate themselves from world problems. Congress passed neutrality laws in the 1930s that forbade Americans from selling arms to belligerent nations or intervening militarily in foreign wars. Neutrality suited the mood of the nation, as public opinion polls taken in 1939 showed that while 80 percent of Americans were sympathetic to the Allies, 90 percent opposed American involvement in the war.[1] With this in mind, FDR did what he could to help the Allies, short of entering the war. After Congress lifted the prohibition on selling arms, FDR came up with several plans for supplying the Allies with the arms and provisions they needed while still claiming American neutrality. The most significant of these plans was the 1941 "lend-lease" program in which American supplies were lent or leased to the Allies during the war, and those supplies could be returned or replaced later. Lend-lease required that the Allies transport the materials on their own ships to maintain U.S. neutrality. FDR compared it to lending your garden hose to a neighbor to extinguish his house fire before the fire spread to your house. Isolationists hated lend-lease, but the American public approved. By this time, however, even isolationists in Congress realized that the United States needed to prepare to defend itself and had, in 1940, authorized additional military spending and the first peacetime military draft.

Unfortunately, tons of lend-lease material ended up at the bottom of the Atlantic Ocean. The British lacked sufficient military vessels to protect the convoys of merchant ships that fell prey to German U-boats. Roosevelt then extended the American security zone to Iceland, allowing the U.S. Navy to escort ships halfway across the Atlantic. This put American ships in the line of fire of German U-boats and made neutral status harder to claim. Still, it would not be Germany that pulled the United States into the war.

In the United States, men received a number when they registered for the draft, and that number was also on a piece of paper contained in a blue capsule in a large glass bowl. Two weeks after the first round of registrations, a blindfolded Secretary of the Navy Frank Knox reached into the bowl to pick a capsule containing the first draft number, which he handed to President Roosevelt, who read the number to the national audience listening on the radio. According to the chalkboard, #158 was the first number, and all men holding that number had to report to local induction centers. Library of Congress, LC-USZ62-134231

This U.S. naval task group presents a formidable armada, December 1944.
National Archives, 80-G-301351

Trouble from the Land of the Rising Sun

Meanwhile, all was not pacific in the Pacific as the Japanese assembled their own empire. Japan's victory over Russia in 1905 gave Japan more confidence and influence in the Far East, which it tested in the 1930s by seizing the Chinese region of Manchuria. Manchuria had natural resources the island nation of Japan lacked, and its conquest was Japan's first step in acquiring by force other territories in the Pacific and domination of the Far East.

The United States protested Japan's actions in China, without much success. FDR then ordered the navy's Pacific Fleet transferred from California to Hawaii as a precautionary measure. The United States and Japan would continue negotiations over China until December 1941, but in the meantime the United States embargoed sales of one vital material after another (such as steel and oil) to Japan, which forced the Japanese to look elsewhere in the Pacific for supplies. After renouncing treaties it had made with democratic countries in the West, Japan allied itself with Germany and Italy in September 1940—an ominous sign. As relations between the United States and Japan deteriorated, Japan planned an attack on the Pacific Fleet that would eliminate the American threat in the Pacific. That attack came at Pearl Harbor on December 7, 1941, "a date," FDR declared, "which will live in infamy."

Sixteen-inch guns of the USS Iowa *firing during battle drill in the Pacific, ca. 1944.* National Archives 80-G-59493

Ships in the harbor and planes at the airfields both suffered crippling damage as a result of the Japanese attack on Pearl Harbor. Smoke billows from a burning battleship on Battleship Row on December 7. National Archives, III-SC-5904

Pearl Harbor

American cryptologists had cracked Japan's secret diplomatic code in December 1940. Deciphered messages confirmed that the Japanese would not abandon China, and that if the United States had not yielded by November 1941, something was going to happen. American authorities guessed the Japanese would hit the Philippines, thus the military commanders at Pearl Harbor in Hawaii prepared for acts of sabotage on the ground, rather than an aerial bombardment. Pearl Harbor readied itself for attack, just not the kind the Japanese had in mind.

By December 7, 1941, a Japanese fleet moved across the Pacific without being detected. Aircraft carriers stopped less than three hundred miles north of Hawaii, and at 6:00 a.m., the first of two waves of planes took off for Pearl Harbor. As the first wave neared the island, radar operators picked up the signal, but their report was ignored by an inexperienced officer who was expecting a flight of American planes from California. No warnings were issued, and so Pearl Harbor was caught unaware.

By 9:45 a.m., Japanese planes had bombed and torpedoed the battle fleet in the harbor and attacked nearby airfields. Six U.S. battleships were sunk, and others were heavily damaged, while several lighter vessels were also sunk or damaged. Over two hundred planes were destroyed or damaged, and the bombing and debris on the airfields made it difficult for U.S. pilots to get serviceable planes in the sky during the attack. In addition to devastating material losses, more than two thousand servicemen and civilians were killed, and over a thousand more were wounded in the attack. Tragically, many servicemen were trapped aboard ships, such as the USS Arizona, that sank too quickly for rescue efforts to succeed.

Wreckage of planes is collected in the aftermath. National Archives, 80-G-32896

Arsenal of Democracy

"To have the United States at our side," British Prime Minister Winston Churchill declared, "was to me the greatest joy." Not only did the British now have another ally, but it also had one with abundant resources at its disposal. Yet, seeing America's potential military and industrial greatness took some imagination in December 1941. The country's traditional suspicion of standing armies, not to mention a decade of economic troubles during the Great Depression, left the military in a pitiful condition. As of 1939, the U.S. military ranked only seventeenth in the world, and even then its weapons were outdated, as was the training of its troops. Nor had industry been operating at full capacity during the Depression. Fulfilling FDR's pledge to be the "arsenal of democracy" for itself and its allies thus was going to be an ambitious undertaking.[3]

Liberty ships were not beautiful, nor were they meant to last. But it was quantity, rather than quality, that made the difference in shipping large numbers of troops and supplies overseas. Library of Congress, LC-USZ62-92190

When word of the Japanese attack at Pearl Harbor reached the mainland, Americans were stunned. All commitments to isolationism were forgotten. Congress granted FDR a declaration of war against Japan on December 8, which prompted Japan's Axis allies Germany and Italy to declare war on the United States. The United States was now in a two-front global war.

While the attack at Pearl Harbor was damaging to the United States, it ultimately proved fatal to the Japanese. "From the viewpoint of history, no Japanese defeat was as bad for them as their successful attack on Pearl Harbor."[2] Admiral Nagumo, who commanded the attack, decided not to launch a third air strike against the fuel and repair depots on Pearl Harbor, which allowed it to remain a viable base. Nearly all the ships damaged in the harbor eventually were salvaged for the war effort, and the crucial American aircraft carriers away at sea on December 7 remained. As importantly, the attack on American territory galvanized the nation for war as nothing else could have done.

Honolulu Star-Bulletin, *December 8, 1941*

Industry as art. Serious work on a submarine at the Electric Boat Company in Connecticut becomes an artistic pairing of man and machine. National Archives, 80-G-468517

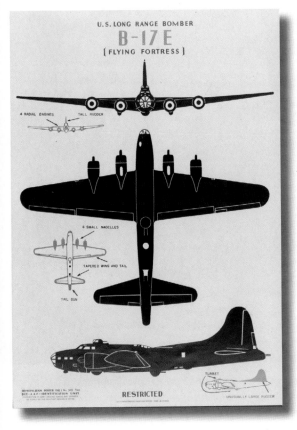

Spotter cards helped soldiers and civilians identify American versus enemy planes based on their outlines and features. Nicknamed the "Flying Fortress," the B-17 was equipped with machine guns to defend itself while on bombing missions, and its ability to survive a beating in the air made it one of the more popular bombers with U.S. airmen. Perhaps the most famous B-17 was the Memphis Belle, *whose crew was the first in the Eighth Air Force to survive twenty-five missions. The* Belle *was the subject of a 1944 documentary by director William Wyler, whose daughter Catherine made a feature film called* Memphis Belle *in 1990.* Library of Congress, LC-USZ62-103751

Once the United States fully turned its attention to wartime production, the results were impressive. When FDR in 1940 called for 50,000 new airplanes a year, critics thought he was crazy. Yet, American industry eventually produced over 96,000 aircraft in 1944 alone. The key to America's industrial success was mass production. Henry Kaiser, for example, found that the secret to building Liberty ships quickly was training workers for a particular task, prefabricating sections of the ships, and then welding the sections together in the shipyard. The production time for Liberty ships at Kaiser shrunk from a month to an astonishing four days, thus explaining why many of the 2,700 Liberty ships floated during the war came from Kaiser Shipyards in California. Assembly lines at the Ford Motor Company's massive Willow Run plant in Michigan produced similar results and manufactured almost half of the 18,000 B-24 bombers produced during the war. Kaiser, however, was also innovative in the treatment of his workers by hiring women of different races, establishing day care facilities for working mothers, and instituting a health care plan still known as Kaiser Permanente.[4]

For the most part, America's production goal was superior quantity, not superior quality. An American-produced Sherman tank, for example, was not the equal of a German tank in terms of tonnage and armament, but the reliable Shermans rarely went into battle alone. Americans built over 88,000 Sherman tanks, while the Germans produced just under 25,000 tanks, which meant that the destruction of one panzer was more crippling to the Germans than an out-of-commission Sherman was to the Americans.[5] In some areas of American industry, though, the quality was equal to the quantity.

Even if it doesn't look like a duck or quack like a duck, it may still be a DUKW. Nicknamed "Ducks," these 2.5-ton amphibious vehicles had standard truck equipment for driving on land but were also fitted with a boat hull and propellers suitable for water use. Ducks were used in nearly all theaters of operation, but were especially valuable for island landings in the Pacific. The term DUKW referred to the vehicle's specifications: D= designed in 1942; U= amphibious; K= all-wheel drive; W= dual rear axles. Today, rehabilitated Ducks are used as sightseeing vehicles in several U.S. cities, including Washington, D.C. National Archives, 208-N-24837

Jeeps first made their appearance during World War II and became beloved pieces of equipment for what they could carry and because they could take on nearly any type of terrain. By the end of the war, American P-51 Mustang fighter planes had no equal in the skies over Europe.

Using all this equipment were the sixteen million Americans who ultimately served in the military during World War II. The vast majority were not professional soldiers; they were ordinary people who volunteered or were drafted into service. Statistically, the average soldier was in his mid-twenties, stood five-feet-eight-inches tall, and weighed about 144 pounds. He had an elementary school education but may not have finished high school. If he served in the infantry, he was most likely white. After induction, he went through basic military training, where he met men from all over the country and made friends with people from all walks of life. And he saw things in battle and shared experiences with these men that bound them together for life.[6]

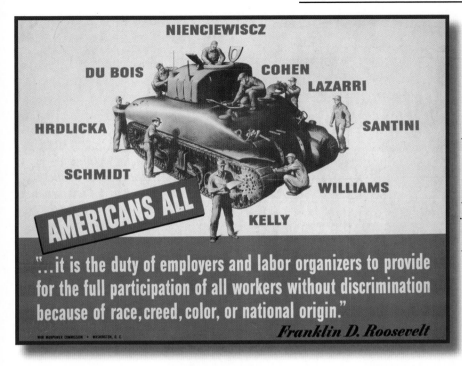

NIENCIEWISCZ
DU BOIS
COHEN
LAZARRI
HRDLICKA
SANTINI
SCHMIDT
WILLIAMS
KELLY

AMERICANS ALL

"...it is the duty of employers and labor organizers to provide for the full participation of all workers without discrimination because of race, creed, color, or national origin."

Franklin D. Roosevelt

WAR MANPOWER COMMISSION • WASHINGTON, D. C.

Wartime conditions forced many people to—at least temporarily—abandon their racial and ethnic prejudices on behalf of the war effort. The necessity of working with people different from themselves opened many people's eyes about their commonalities rather than their differences. Library of Congress, LC-USZC4-4265

Life on the Home Front

Being the arsenal of democracy required people to work in the fields and the factories, and once men started entering the military in large numbers, America experienced a labor shortage for the first time since the start of the Great Depression. All sorts of Americans came forward to fill the gap; some prompted by patriotism, others by the promise of higher wages. Some groups were met with doubts or outright hostility, but as FDR pointed out in 1942, "We can no longer afford to indulge in such prejudice."[7]

People who normally would have been considered less employable in the industrial sector became valuable workers because of the labor shortages caused by the war. By 1943, 200,000 blind and disabled Americans were working in defense industries.[32] *Some literally found their occupational niche when it was discovered they could fit INSIDE an airplane wing to do finishing work.* Franklin D. Roosevelt Library, 66113 (37)

This poster takes a friendly jab at all those men who did not think women were up to the task of working in war industries. Library of Congress, LC-USZC4-5597

Women entered the workforce in unprecedented numbers during the war. Many of these women had always worked out of economic necessity but found that the wages paid in war industries were much higher than those for domestic workers. But others entered the workforce for the first time. Sometimes these women had to be coaxed into it with reassurances that factory work was not that much different than housework. "If you've followed recipes exactly in making cakes, you can learn to load shell," proclaimed one billboard. Once in the workplace, though, most women found the work fulfilling, enjoyed the camaraderie of their fellow females, liked the pay, and felt they were participating in the war effort. At the height of production in 1943 and 1944, nearly half of adult women in America were working.[8]

While it may look like these women are polishing spotted Easter eggs, they are actually checking the lines of noses destined for A-20 attack bombers at a Douglas Aircraft facility in Long Beach, California. The glass is just reflecting lights from the factory ceiling.
National Archives, 208-AA-352QQ-5

WOMEN IN AIRCRAFT INDUSTRY

In October, 1941, there were 1900 productive women employees in aircraft plants. In July, 1942, only 9 months later, this number had grown to 39,000—nearly a 2000% increase.

1900   OCT. '41

2500   NOV. '41

6900   JAN. '42

16000   MCH. '42

39000   JULY '42

SOURCE: AERONAUTICAL CHAMBER OF COMMERCE OF AMERICA

This graph illustrates the huge jump in one year of the number of women employed in the aircraft industry, which employed more women than nearly any other defense industry.[33] The Solar Blast (September 1942), Author's collection

Other women put on uniforms of a different sort and joined the military. Although no branch of the U.S. military accepted women on the same status as men, all created women's auxiliary units for additional "manpower." The army created the Women's Army Auxiliary Corps (WAAC), which later dropped the "Auxiliary" to become the WACs. The navy appropriately had the WAVES (Women Accepted for Volunteer Emergency Service), the Coast Guard the SPARS (Semper Paratus, Always Ready), and the air corps the WASPs (Women Airforce Service Pilots). Only the Marines avoided clever acronyms for their women. Regardless which of the service branches they joined, by the end of the war, the thousands of women who had enlisted in the military had done practically every non-combat job available, which proved their competency and freed up more men for frontline duty.

Still other women contributed to the war effort by serving as military nurses around the world, entertaining soldiers at United Service Organizations (USO) centers at home and abroad, toiling as "government girl" clerical workers in Washington, D.C., or by joining the American Red Cross. By volunteering for more typically "feminine" jobs, these women faced less gender prejudice than industrial workers or military women, but their roles were no less important.

While the United States fought for the preservation of freedom abroad, some Americans waged an additional battle to secure their own equality at home. World War II—era America was still a segregated place, where blacks often were denied equal access to places and opportunities enjoyed by whites. Picking up on the "V for Victory" symbols used to support the war effort generally, many blacks fought a "Double V" campaign to advance their own cause during the war. Early in 1941, before America even entered the war, blacks began protesting discrimination in hiring practices in defense industries and threatened to march

For your country's sake today—

For your own sake tomorrow

Posters like this one encouraged women to do their patriotic duty by volunteering but also made sure to portray them as every inch the lady. Becoming a Marine, for example, did not mean giving up one's femininity—Elizabeth Arden created a new shade of lipstick called Montezuma Red to match the red trim on the uniforms worn by women Marines.[34] National Archives, 44-PA-820

on Washington if something was not done. President Roosevelt feared the negative publicity and established the Fair Employment Practices Commission to investigate complaints of discrimination. As a result, blacks on the home front enjoyed employment opportunities previously denied them. This also applied to black women, who essentially fought a triple "V" campaign to combat racial and gender discrimination.

Future poet Maya Angelou, for example, fought during the war to become the first black streetcar conductor in San Francisco.[9] Many other black women left domestic work for higher wages in factories.

American pilots back at their base in the Mediterranean compare notes on the day's mission, February 1944. National Archives, 208-MO-18H-22051

Tuskegee Airmen

The military reflected the tone of the times and segregated blacks into their own units, which were usually limited to non-combat duties. Black servicemen were eager to prove themselves during the war, and perhaps no units distinguished themselves as much as the 99th Fighter Squadron and 332nd Fighter Group, better known collectively as the Tuskegee Airmen. Training at Moton Air Field near the historic Tuskegee Institute in Alabama, the program began as an experiment in training blacks to fly. The airmen got the chance to prove themselves as air support during the Allied landing at Anzio, Italy, and performed so well that they were assigned to escort bombers in Europe. The planes of the 332nd Fighter Group were painted red on the tails to distinguish their unit. White pilots were initially skeptical of their black counterparts, but once the 332nd began building a nearly perfect record for escorting their bombers safely, white pilots soon forgot their prejudices and actually requested "The Red Tails."[10] *This was both attributable to the skill of the Tuskegee Airmen and the fact that their leader, Benjamin O. Davis Jr., directed his pilots to protect the bomber rather than go hunting for enemy aircraft.*[11] *The Tuskegee Airmen as a segregated aviation unit ceased to exist after the Air Force was integrated in 1949.*

When this photograph of Benjamin O. Davis Jr. (1912–2002) was taken in January 1942, the then-Captain Davis was just weeks away from receiving his pilot's wings. A West Point graduate, Davis was one of the first cadets to join the pioneering aviation program for African Americans at Tuskegee, Alabama. Davis led both the 99th Pursuit Squadron and 332nd Fighter Group, and distinguished himself with his natural leadership abilities. After commanding other air units during peacetime, he again saw combat during the Korean War. Davis became the first African American general in the Air Force and was promoted to lieutenant general before his retirement in 1970. President Bill Clinton awarded Davis a fourth star in 1998. Davis is buried in Arlington National Cemetery, as is his father, Benjamin O. Davis Sr., the Army's first black general. National Archives, 208-FS-872-3

Further War Restrictions on Telephone Service

The War Production Board, on March 25, 1943, ordered further restrictions on the installation of telephone service. The purpose of the Order is to save additional critical materials, such as copper, rubber, steel and tin, which are urgently needed for the fighting forces. Of particular interest to all telephone customers is that part of the Order which provides that:

"All service, involving exchange central office equipment and/or exchange line plant, installed or reconnected on and after April 15, 1943, shall be on an interim basis only, that is, subject to regrading and disconnection — "

This means that customers for whom such service is installed on and after April 15, 1943, or who have their telephone service moved to a new address on and after that date may later have to share their lines with others or may have to give up their telephones entirely if the facilities are required to provide telephones for persons engaged in direct defense or charged with responsibility for public health, welfare or security as classified by the War Production Board in the Order.

While these restrictions may cause inconvenience to some people—part of the essential sacrifices for Victory—we are sure of your understanding and co-operation and we pledge on our part continuing effort to keep our service up to the highest possible standard.

Southern California Telephone Company

(A) 4-43

Because most metals were needed for the war effort, Americans at home had to accept a variety of unexpected changes. Copper was a particularly precious metal in 1943, as telephone customers in Southern California discovered. Likewise, 1943 pennies were made from zinc-coated steel to divert copper supplies for military use. Even after sixty years, the steel penny is still visibly different from its copper cousins of 1942 and 1944. Forty copper pennies were minted accidentally in 1943, and in 1996 one of these rare coins sold for over $82,000![35] So a 1943 copper is literally worth a pretty penny. Author's collection

Even with enough workers to man the factories and fields, getting the materials needed to make war supplies caused some concern. War industries needed more and more of everything to produce guns, planes, and ammunition. Trouble was, some of the raw materials, like rubber, came from places in war zones, or ships could not be spared to transport enough for both military and civilian use. The answer was rationing, recycling, and "making do" on the home front. To meet production quotas for airplanes and military vehicles, most of the automotive industry stopped producing cars for civilian use and retooled their factories for government contracts. That meant that the last new car a driver bought would be the last new car he could buy for a while. Not that it mattered much because rubber supplies were being diverted to military equipment, and he had to drive sparingly to make his tires last as long as possible. If he happened to have a spare tire, the government hoped he would turn it in to be recycled for the war effort. But even with a working car and decent tires, his driving habits were determined by how many gallons of gasoline his ration coupon allowed because gasoline was being rationed as well. By the end of the war, sugar, coffee, and meat were all subject to rationing, forcing housewives to be creative in their cooking. Silk was diverted from making ladies' stockings to making parachutes, and a banana shortage forced the makers

of Twinkies to switch to (the now familiar) vanilla rather than banana cream filling. Metal supplies largely went to war industries, and citizens were encouraged to donate to collection drives all the scrap metal they had. First Lady Eleanor Roosevelt used her newspaper column to encourage recycling, pointing out that the metal in an unused wash pail could make three bayonets.[12]

Life on the home front changed in more ways than just rationing. To make urban centers and coastlines less visible, people in cities and on both coasts followed blackout conditions, which meant extinguishing porch lights, covering windows to hide inside lights, and driving cars without the headlights on. Civil defense volunteers were responsible for making sure their neighborhoods were safe from enemy attack.

It's fat collection day for children in Roanoke, Virginia! Recycling rubber and metals makes sense, but cooking fat? Fats contained glycerine, which could be used to make gunpowder and explosives for military use. So housewives were encouraged to save their waste fats for government collection and recycling. By 1943, about ninety million pounds of household fats were being collected a year.[36] Franklin D. Roosevelt Library, 65701 (31)

With gasoline rationing and blackouts in effect, millions of Americans went to the movies each week, but even here they could not escape the war. Many Hollywood films now centered on patriotic war themes, like Thirty Seconds Over Tokyo (1944), starring Spencer Tracy, which followed the pilots who went on the daring Doolittle bombing raid over Tokyo in 1942. Documentary films, such as Frank Capra's influential series Why We Fight, were used to educate men off to the front lines and explain to the folks back home why the American war aims were worth the sacrifice. Library of Congress, LC-USZC4-3698

Gasoline was rationed during the war, and the government determined how much each car owner would receive based on various criteria, such as the driver's occupation and if driving was being done for war-related activities. Gasoline coupons like these were then issued, and drivers could fill up with only as much gasoline as their coupons allowed them. Author's collection

You Can't Build A Substantial V Out of Turtles!

DAWDLING PRODUCERS

Before he was Dr. Seuss, the beloved author of children's books, Theodor Geisel was Dr. Seuss, the editorial cartoonist. During the war, Dr. Seuss drew for a publication called PM, *and his cartoons encouraged war bond purchases and poked fun at rationing, isolationists, and those who thought that victory would happen without any sacrifice. The characters Dr. Seuss drew for* PM *eventually became the characters that taught similar life lessons in his children's books. Do you see "Yertle the Turtle" in this "V"?* Mandeville Special Collections Library, University of California, San Diego

Savings bonds came in a variety of denominations, making them as accessible to the school child as to the millionaire. Each of the postal war savings stamps in these sets only cost ten cents, and when an album of stamps had reached the price of a regular Treasury bond, the stamps could be traded for a bond. Author's collection

Before being evacuated to permanent camps, internees reported to temporary assembly centers. These internees had just arrived at the Santa Anita racetrack in California, and many of them would be housed in stalls from which the horses had only recently been removed. National Archives, 210-G-3B-414

This portrait of Corporal Jimmie Shohara was taken at Manzanar Relocation Center in California while he was on leave visiting his parents. Ironically, they were still interned as "enemy aliens." Library of Congress, LC-DIG-ppprs-00074

Photographer Dorothea Lange captures the sadness of two young Japanese Americans packed for relocation in May 1942. National Archives, 210-G-3C-310

Executive Order 9066

On February 19, 1942, President Roosevelt signed Executive Order 9066. In the name of national security, the order authorized the U.S. military to exclude "any and all persons" from living in designated areas. Without specifically saying so, E.O. 9066 was directed at Japanese immigrants and their American-born children, who already had faced years of legal and racial discrimination, especially on the West Coast. After Japan bombed Pearl Harbor, suspicions against Japanese Americans increased, and with the president's approval, over 120,000 people of Japanese ancestry were forced to relocate to remote internment camps in the West. Restricted to taking only what they could carry, many lost homes and businesses, as well as their personal liberty. The internment camps were surrounded by barbed-wire fences, the housing could not protect the residents from great variations in weather conditions, and the food was very different from the traditional Japanese diet. Still, internees did what they could to adapt to their new lives by joining sports teams, working in gardens, and organizing classes.

In 1943, the military began recruiting soldiers from the internment camps. Residents were given questionnaires to determine their loyalty and if they would be willing to serve in the U.S. military. While some refused to answer these questions, others completed the questionnaires and joined the 25,000 Japanese Americans who served during the war. Two units of Japanese-American soldiers, the 100th Infantry Battalion and 442nd Regimental Combat Team, served with distinction in Europe with a "go for broke" attitude that led the combined unit to become one of the more decorated in U.S. history.

Although the last camps closed in 1946, many internees had been released by early 1945 after a 1944 Supreme Court decision that the government could not forcibly hold American citizens on the grounds of military necessity. They were given $25 and transportation, and were expected to pick up the pieces of their lives. In the years after the war, some internees took legal action against the United States for their incarceration, and congressional legislation in the 1980s both acknowledged the mistake of internment and provided $20,000 in reparations to each surviving internee.[13]

The Atlantic Theater

From the beginning, aircraft played an enormous role in World War II. After the Battle of Britain, the RAF began to return the favor by bombing Nazi military targets in Germany and occupied France, a practice the Americans continued when they joined the war. Some strategists hoped that air bombardments alone would weaken the German war machine, making a land invasion unnecessary. Precision bombing, however, was far from precise, and targets were often missed. Military objectives were sometimes close to civilian populations, so planners had to accept inflicting destruction on cultural centers and causing civilian casualties. Fire bombings of Dresden, Germany, and Tokyo, Japan, in 1945 were particularly controversial for the damage suffered by civilian centers.

Flying bombing missions could be equally deadly for Allied pilots and crew due to flak from anti-aircraft guns, being shot down by the Luftwaffe, or experiencing mechanical difficulties and having to bail out over enemy territory. Furthermore, not until the B-29s began flying in 1944 were planes heated or pressurized, meaning that once the planes reached an altitude of 20,000 feet, the temperatures inside could plunge to -30°F or lower. The crew also had to wear oxygen masks at that height or risk losing consciousness within minutes. Nearly 40,000 Americans were killed in combat missions during the air war, and the Eighth Air Force took particularly high casualties of 26,000 men.[14] Thus, the damage inflicted on the Axis came at a high price for the Allies.

Precision bombing also required precision in the air. In this horrifying photograph, two American planes have flown out of formation over Germany, with the lower plane now in the line of fire from the plane in which this photo was taken. Bombs have already sheared off part of the tail wing, while another heads directly toward the fuselage. Franklin D. Roosevelt Library, 74201301

North Africa became a military objective early in the war because Mussolini hoped to emulate Hitler's success in empire building in Europe by adding African territory to his imperial balance sheet. The British, however, were concerned that Mussolini's actions in Africa threatened their access to the Mediterranean Sea and their interests in the Middle East. British troops subdued the Italians in North Africa with relative ease, only to discover that Hitler was diverting resources there to neutralize the British threat in the Mediterranean. Field Marshal Erwin Rommel and his mechanized Afrika Korps proved a more formidable opponent than the Italians, and the Americans under General Eisenhower faced their first land campaigns in the Atlantic Theater fighting with British forces in North Africa in late 1942. National Archives, III-SC-179564

The air war, then, had to complement a ground war, which had begun in North Africa as the Axis and Allies wrestled for control of the Mediterranean. When Allied victory looked assured in North Africa and the German offensive bogged down at Stalingrad in the USSR in 1942, Churchill and FDR met at Casablanca in January 1943 to plan the next Allied move. Although the destruction of Germany remained the primary objective, more troops would be moved into the Pacific for further offensives there. Meanwhile the Allies would invade the so-called "soft underbelly" of Europe through Sicily and Italy to take some pressure off the USSR. This delay would allow the Allies to organize their combined resources for a later invasion of France.

Josef Stalin of the Soviet Union, Franklin Roosevelt of the United States, and Winston Churchill of Great Britain meet at Tehran, Iran, in December 1943. Unlike the Axis nations who operated independently of each other, the "Big Three" nations worked together to plan military campaigns to achieve common war aims. The United States and Great Britain developed a particularly close relationship during the war and united their fighting forces for truly Allied operations in the west. Library of Congress, LC-USZ62-91957

While each theater of operation presented its own challenges for fighting, the Italian campaign was notorious for the steep and rugged terrain. "The country is shockingly beautiful," wrote journalist Ernie Pyle (1900-1945), "and just as shockingly hard to capture from the enemy."[37] National Archives, III-SC-205289

The Italian campaign began in the summer of 1943. After their conquest of Sicily, the Allies invaded the Italian mainland at Salerno. By the time they arrived, opposition forces within Italy had overthrown Mussolini, and Hitler had increased the German forces there. Although the new Italian government surrendered to the Allies in September, the Germans held the mountains, which meant that actually conquering Italy would be a rough and costly campaign. Attempting to quicken the pace, the Allies made an amphibious landing in January 1944 at Anzio, located behind the main German lines. What could have been a surprise attack against the Germans resulted in the Allies being pinned on the beaches by German artillery on the high ground. As Allied forces battled Germans elsewhere in Italy, those at Anzio eventually broke free and raced for Rome, which fell on June 4, 1944. Italy itself had not been won, however, and the Allies would continue their agonizing and bloody advances northward until spring 1945.

The fall of Rome was momentous news, but the world's attention in June 1944 turned to the beaches of Normandy on the French coast—the long-awaited cross-channel invasion of Europe was on. For months the Allies had been assembling supplies, training troops, planting rumors to confuse the Nazis, and planning the largest amphibious landing of the war.

"Didn't we meet at Cassino?"

"Didn't we meet at Cassino?" asks cartoonist Bill Mauldin's character Willie, as he confronts a German soldier. The battles of Monte Cassino in 1944 formed part of the brutal Italian campaign, in which some fighting in the mountains did bring opposing soldiers into close contact. Based on his own war experiences, Mauldin's (1921–2003) cartoons reflected the hard reality and ironic humor of front-line infantrymen, giving the folks back home a sense of what the "dogfaces" were going through. Library of Congress, LC-DIG-ppmsca-03236

A military is made up of more than just infantrymen on the front lines or Marines storming the beaches. During World War II, several men served in a support capacity for every one man in combat. Important support staff included men like William W. Scudder (1904–1965), who served as a chief pharmacist's mate in the U.S. Navy during the war. He wore his dress uniform for his portrait but wore the jacket (pictured) on more ordinary occasions. Like many of his comrades in arms, Scudder became a father during the war but was not able to see his daughter Sharon until she was over a year old. Courtesy of Sharon Beeman 41

General Dwight D. Eisenhower talks to American paratroopers as they prepare for the D-Day invasion of France on June 6, 1944. The #23 around Lt. Wallace Strobel's neck indicates his plane number.[38] National Archives, III-SC-194399

On the morning of June 6, 1944, an armada of ships, carrying more than one hundred thousand Allied soldiers, set off across the English Channel to storm the German positions on the beaches of Normandy. Ten thousand paratroopers had already been dropped behind enemy lines to provide cover in the interior, although the drops had not gone as smoothly as planned. British and Canadian forces found little opposition on their beach landings, but the Americans faced stiff resistance at Omaha Beach. German machine gun fire from pillboxes on the cliffs above slaughtered troops exiting their landing crafts in the water and mowed soldiers down on the beaches. "As our boat touched sand and the ramp went down," remembered Private Harry Parley, "I became a visitor to hell."[15] Late in the day, the sheer number of troops and more precise naval shelling allowed the Americans to take the beachhead and begin their advance inland.

The difficult fighting only continued as the Allies fought their way through the countryside and villages (like Saint-Lô) of occupied France. Allied troops, however, continued to push the Germans ever eastward. With assistance from the Free French, General George S. Patton's forces liberated Paris in August 1944 while in hot pursuit of the retreating Germans. By September, Belgium, Luxembourg, and much of France were in Allied hands, with the next stop being the German border itself.

But the Allies moved more quickly than supply lines could stretch, forcing General Dwight D. Eisenhower to reorganize before beginning another advance. This gave the Germans time to mount one last major offensive, pushing through Allied lines in the Ardennes forest in southern Belgium, creating a bulge in the Allied line. The speed of the German attack caught Allied forces in the town of Bastogne in December. When ordered by the Germans to surrender, American commander General Anthony McAuliffe refused with the one-word answer "Nuts!" which had to be translated for the confused German messenger as "go to hell."[16] After sustaining heavy casualties at the Bulge, the Allies finally pushed the Germans back to their original lines. While the British and Americans advanced on the western front, Soviet troops plowed through eastern Europe. By the time the "Big Three"—FDR, Churchill, and Stalin—met at Yalta in February 1945 for another summit, the Soviets had advanced to within fifty miles of Berlin.

After watching in horror as German troops marched down the Champs Élysées to occupy France four years earlier, Parisians delighted to see the Americans parade through a liberated Paris in August 1944. "We all got kissed until we were literally red in the face," wrote Ernie Pyle.[39] National Archives, 208-AA-196T-15658PPA

On March 7, 1945, the Allies crossed the last remaining bridge over the Rhine River at Remagen and met up with the Russians at the Elbe River on April 25. When FDR suddenly died of a cerebral hemorrhage on April 12, Hitler for a moment thought the tide of the war could turn with the new, untested President Harry Truman in command. By April 30, however, Hitler knew his supposed thousand-year Reich was on the verge of collapse, after slightly more than a decade in existence. He committed suicide in an underground bunker in Berlin. Seven days later, German representatives agreed to an unconditional surrender, and people in Allied nations around the world celebrated V-E Day—Victory in Europe Day.

True, the war had ended in the Atlantic Theater . . . but it still raged in the Pacific.

A cathedral statue surveys her ruined city of Dresden, Germany, after Allied fire bombings in early 1945. Library of Congress, LC-USZ62-94453

Victorious American generals sit for a group portrait in 1945, including George S. Patton (seated, second from left), Dwight Eisenhower (seated, middle), and Omar Bradley (to right of Eisenhower). National Archives, 208-YE-182

A box of gold wedding rings is powerful testimony to the number of people imprisoned and exterminated for being objectionable in the eyes of Nazi authorities. This is just one box of confiscated rings, from one location. There were many more boxes filled at many more facilities over the course of the war. National Archives, 208-YE-1B-23

Still wearing their prison uniforms, inmates liberated from the Wöbbelin concentration camp by the Eighty-second Airborne in May 1945 show the extent of the physical and psychological torture they endured at the hands of the Nazis. National Archives, 208-YE-1B-4

The Holocaust

As Allied troops swept through Germany in spring 1945, they made a horrifying discovery. The Nazis had erected labor and concentration camps for the imprisonment and slaughter of Jews and other "undesirables," such as gypsies, Soviet prisoners of war, communists, homosexuals, and the handicapped.

News that the Nazis were murdering European Jews in concentration camps first reached the United States in August 1942. However, false rumors about German atrocities had surfaced during World War I, and many were suspicious of these new accusations. Some people could simply not imagine such horror stories could be true. Furthermore, with millions of soldiers and civilians dying worldwide in the war, conflicting accounts of the deaths of thousands of Jews at a time failed to make front-page news. "We knew in a general way that the Jews were being persecuted," one intelligence officer remembered, "but few if any comprehended the appalling magnitude of it. It wasn't sufficiently real to stand out from the general brutality and slaughter which is war."[17]

Could America have done something about the Holocaust? Some historians claim that the United States could have relaxed strict immigra-

tion laws for Jewish refugees. There is evidence that anti-Jewish prejudice in the State Department led to stalling tactics in issuing entrance visas to Jews fleeing Europe, but public opinion in the United States at the time was also against allowing more refugees into the country. Other critics suggest that American airplanes could have bombed the railroad lines to the concentration camps, or ground troops could have staged rescue attempts. High-altitude bombings often missed specific targets, however, and the Allies could not physically rescue camp victims until ground forces entered Germany in 1945. The War Refugee Board, established in 1944, did rescue 200,000 Jews, but not before an estimated five to six million Jews were exterminated simply for being Jewish.[18] Millions of non-Jews also perished during the war, both in organized concentration camps and by general mistreatment at the hands of the Nazis.

Upon liberating the Ohrdruf camp in April 1945, General Eisenhower required U.S. soldiers in the vicinity to tour the camp. "We are told that the American soldier does not know what he is fighting for," he explained. "Now, at least, he will know what he is fighting against."[19]

Soldiers on the front lines rarely had the time or opportunity to eat a hot, tasty meal. Chow often came in the form of "C" or "K" rations, which were packaged meals of various caloric values. The troops (top) have a K-ration lunch on a ship in the English Channel in June 1944, while the G.I.'s (bottom) line up for provisions in Belgium in January 1945. K rations may have had an adequate number of calories to keep a body going, but most veterans would confirm that you could only eat so much canned beef. National Archives, 26-G-2403; III-SC-198849

Getting mail from home was an important lifeline for the fighting forces, for news and for confirmation that they had not been forgotten while away. As the "army examiner" stamp on the envelope demonstrates, however, letters from soldiers were checked first to be sure they did not contain any information that would help the enemy should the letter fall into the wrong hands. The censors would literally cut out restricted information in letters. Even under those conditions, the feelings of the letters moved one censor to recall that "I read some of the greatest prose in the English language, written by eighteen-year-old kids who couldn't spell."[40] Author's collection

Alan Waterhouse.
Author's collection

The range of what soldiers did in their leisure time ran from "holy" to "holy cow!" The bombed shell of Coventry Cathedral in England still provided U.S. soldiers a place to worship in May 1943. Across the globe at Guadalcanal, these servicemen demonstrated that collecting pictures of their sweethearts and Hollywood pin-up girls kept boredom at bay and perhaps inspired a sweet dream or two. National Archives, 111-SC-206681, 80-G-280693

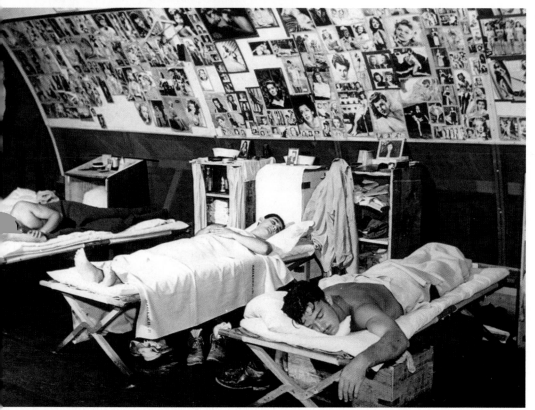

The Pacific Theater

Within hours of the bombing of Pearl Harbor in December 1941, the Japanese also attacked American air bases in the Philippines, inflicting significant damage. American troops under General Douglas MacArthur escaped to the Bataan peninsula and nearby island of Corregidor, but they could not hold out indefinitely against the Japanese forces that had landed in the Philippines. FDR ordered MacArthur to Australia, and not long after the general vowed "I shall return," nearly 70,000 American and Filipino soldiers were taken prisoner in 1942.[20] The number of prisoners overwhelmed the Japanese (who did not have a tradition of respecting those who surrendered), and they

Then, as now, soldiers in the field appreciated any entertainment that came their way, and especially if it came in the form of pretty girls. This view only captured a portion of the ten thousand happy soldiers who attended the Copacabana All Girl Review near Marseilles, France, in 1945. National Archives, III-SC-210796

From directional signs on Tarawa in the Pacific, to a World War I memorial in Sicily in the Mediterranean, servicemen who had seen horrific fighting could still display a sense of humor. National Archives, 80-G-476304, III-SC-179879

were marched to prison camps. Weakened by disease and malnourishment, and abused by their Japanese captors, thousands of prisoners died or were executed along the way, giving the journey the well-deserved title the "Bataan Death March." The Japanese followed up their success in the Philippines by seizing other Allied territory in the Pacific, including Guam, Wake Island, and parts of New Guinea. Upon taking Burma, the Japanese closed the Burma Road, forcing the Allies to use other routes to supply Chiang Kai-shek's forces in China.

Japan's winning streak ended at the Battles of Coral Sea and Midway in May and June 1942. Coral Sea marked the first time a battle was fought solely by planes from aircraft carriers, and while not a victory for the Allies, they inflicted enough damage to put the Japanese at a disadvantage at the Battle of Midway. The victory at Midway kept the Japanese out of range of Pearl Harbor, and with the Japanese loss of four aircraft carriers, naval superiority in the Pacific shifted to the Allies. The Japanese did capture Attu in the Aleutian Islands but without much effect.

After Midway, both the Americans and Japanese tried to capture Guadalcanal island in August 1942. The Marines landed with little opposition and took the enemy airstrip, but the Japanese recognized the island's strategic importance and sent reinforcements. The fight for Guadalcanal raged for six bloody months before the Japanese abandoned the island in February 1943. The heat and humidity in the jungles of Guadalcanal made for brutal fighting conditions for the Marines, while the navy suffered heavy losses in the waters surrounding the island. Still, Guadalcanal proved another turning point in that the Japanese had not been able to stop the Allies on land any more than they had the navy at Midway, and notions of Japanese invincibility disappeared after Guadalcanal.[21]

Once the Japanese cut off major transportation routes in the China-Burma-India theater, new roads were constructed and supplies airlifted "over the hump" of mountains to U.S. allies in China. But even by 1945, convoys still faced unusual routes, like this road at Annan, China. National Archives, 111-SC-208807

To remove the heavily entrenched Japanese from island fortifications, American troops often had to resort to using flamethrowers to burn the enemy out. This scene featured the army's Seventh Division on Kwajalein in 1944, but it was just a prelude to the fighting Marines saw on Iwo Jima and Okinawa in 1945. National Archives, III-SC-212770

Japanese strategy then turned to defending the islands that lay between the Allies and Japan, forcing the Allies to expend enormous energy to extract the Japanese from their entrenched positions. Taking each occupied island was not viable, so the Allies instead engaged in "island hopping," by conquering only the strategic islands necessary to support an eventual invasion of Japan itself. From Tarawa to Kwajalein, to Wake Island, to the Philippine Sea, to Saipan, Tinian, and Guam, the Allies landed on one Pacific island after another and faced tenacious Japanese defenders and often brutal conditions. But by October 1944, the way was clear for MacArthur and his troops to set out for the Philippines. Fighting for control of Manila took months and nearly destroyed the city, but as good as his word, MacArthur had returned. Just days after MacArthur waded ashore at Leyte Gulf, "the greatest naval struggle of all time" took place there.[22] The Japanese tried yet again to destroy the U.S. Pacific Fleet but ultimately succeeded in further crippling their own. Of the five hundred planes lost by the Japanese in the three-day naval battle, a number were lost on purpose. Japanese suicide (or *kamikaze*) pilots began to deliberately fly their planes into American ships as a new and deadly weapon.

Correspondent Ernie Pyle could have been describing this mass of supplies on Okinawa in 1945 when he wrote, "you can take your pick of K-rations or lumber or bombs, and you'd find enough of each to feed a city, build one, or blow it up."[41] National Archives, 26-G-4426

General Douglas MacArthur returning to the Philippines in October 1944.
National Archives, III-SC-407101

In a war that produced many remarkable images, this image by Associated Press photographer Joe Rosenthal of the second flag raising on Mt. Suribachi, on Iwo Jima, is probably the most famous photograph of the war. The image also inspired artist Felix de Weldon to sculpt the group, and his rendering is the centerpiece of the United States Marine Corps War Memorial (more commonly known as the "Iwo Jima Memorial") in Arlington, Virginia. National Archives, 80-G-413988

Despite their losses in the Pacific, the Japanese strongly resisted Allied invasions, sometimes literally to the last man. On the small island of Iwo Jima, the Japanese had dug in for a fight by constructing an elaborate system of fortified caves capable of withstanding American artillery fire. From their protected and elevated position, the Japanese subjected Marines on the beaches to withering machine gun and artillery fire. The fighting on Iwo Jima was so intense that Admiral Chester Nimitz later remarked that "uncommon valor was a common virtue" for the Marines on the island. Similar resistance and fighting faced the Marines who landed on Okinawa as well. Iwo Jima and Okinawa were considered crucial for providing support bases for the huge B-29 Superfortresses that dropped devastating firebombs on Japan in spring 1945 in preparation for an eventual invasion. But uncommon virtue had cost American forces dearly: 6,000 dead on Iwo Jima, and 12,000 dead on Okinawa. American authorities feared that the casualties would be considerably higher when the Allies invaded Japan itself. As it happened, they never had to find out.

Of the forty-five thousand American Indians who served during World War II, more than four hundred served in the Pacific as "code talkers." Navajos, like the men seen here, communicated with each other in a coded version of their native language. Since the Japanese never cracked the Navajo "code," sensitive information about enemy positions and troop movements could be transmitted securely over the radio. National Archives, 127-MN-69889-B

Death could and did come in an instant for the Marines fighting on Iwo Jima. Bayonet fixed and ready to charge, this Marine from the "Fighting Fourth" was killed on the beach by Japanese sniper fire in February 1945. National Archives, 127-G-109624

How many men fit on the barrel of a captured German 274-mm railroad gun? Twenty-two, if they are from the U.S. Seventh Army. And needless to say they are happier to be ON the barrel itself rather than on the receiving end. National Archives, III-SC-203308

Japan's surrender in August 1945 was cause for Americans to celebrate around the world, including Paris, where joyous G.I.'s hold up a special edition of the Paris Post announcing "JAPS QUIT." The official ceremony on the deck of the USS Missouri in Tokyo Bay on September 2, 1945, was a more solemn occasion, as General Douglas MacArthur signs the formal Japanese surrender document. National Archives, III-SC-210208; 80-G-348366

The Flight of the Enola Gay

German scientists had begun exploring the use of atomic energy for military purposes in the early 1930s, which alarmed refugee scientists from Europe who feared what Hitler would do with such a potentially destructive weapon. This fear prompted scientists like Albert Einstein to convince FDR to begin an atomic program in the United States. Scientists at various research universities studied the physics of making an atomic bomb using a new element called plutonium, while producing enough plutonium fell to the "Manhattan Project" in Oak Ridge, Tennessee. At Los Alamos, New Mexico, a team of scientists under J. Robert Oppenheimer worked on making the bomb a reality. The first successful test of this new weapon

occurred July 16, 1945, well after the European war had ended. The program was kept so secret that Vice President Harry Truman did not even know about it until he was briefed after FDR's death.

But it became Truman's responsibility to decide whether or not to use atomic weapons to force Japan to surrender and, in the process, bring the world into the atomic age. Although the Japanese were by the summer of 1945 clearly fighting a losing battle, they had refused demands to surrender. The next step for the United States was an invasion of the Japanese home islands, and authorities feared the dreadful loss of life for American troops that would inevitably occur. Truman decided to drop the bomb.

A mushroom cloud ascends over 60,000 feet in the air after the atomic bomb nicknamed "Fat Man" was dropped over Nagasaki on August 9, 1945. National Archives, 208-N-43888

The restored cockpit of the Enola Gay at the National Air and Space Museum's Steven F. Udvar-Hazy Center in Virginia. As testament to how controversial the dropping of the atomic bomb remains, the Enola Gay is the only plane on the ground floor of the museum that is raised off the floor (see the visible yellow supports on either side of the plane) to make it less accessible to protestors. Author's collection

On August 6, 1945, the Enola Gay, a B-29 bomber named after the pilot's mother, dropped the first atomic bomb (nicknamed "Little Boy") over the Japanese city of Hiroshima. The blast instantly killed 75,000 people and nearly vaporized the city. When Japan still refused to concede defeat, a second bomb was dropped over Nagasaki on August 9. The Japanese gave up on August 14, and the formal surrender ceremony occurred on September 2, 1945. World War II was officially over.

Truman later claimed he had had no doubts about using atomic weapons to end the war, and most Americans agreed with his decision. Others at the time and in the years since the war, however, have raised questions about America's use of the bomb. Were the Japanese close to surrendering anyway? Should the United States have first issued a more specific warning to the Japanese? Was the second bomb really necessary? All these questions have been debated endlessly since the war, and the debate shows no sign of ending soon. A firestorm of controversy arose in 1995 when sections of the Enola Gay went on display at the National Air and Space Museum in Washington, D.C. Veterans groups clashed with museum curators and historians on viewpoints presented in the proposed exhibit. In the end, the text explained very little beyond the mechanics of the plane itself, but the dispute demonstrated how emotional this subject remains a half-century later.

After the War...

With WWII at an end, the "citizen soldiers" returned home to a world different in many ways from the one they had left. Men who had seen combat returned bearing the emotional scars of war, leaving them changed by the experience. Most refused to talk about the ugly aspects of the war because no one who had not been there would truly understand. Married men whose wives entered the workforce or had to be more independent homemakers during the war sometimes found their women had changed as well. "He had left a shrinking violet," one woman remembered, but came "home to a very strong oak tree." Not all husbands welcomed the change. Other couples had married impulsively in the excitement of wartime. Not surprisingly, the divorce rate in America was higher in 1946 than any time before the 1970s.[23]

The end of the war also meant that millions of women in the workforce in 1945 were laid off since industry was no longer producing at a frenzied pace and returning soldiers supplied the labor force.

Some women were happy to return to their homes, but many had come to appreciate the independence and good wages industrial jobs had provided.

But soldiers also returned to a country no longer plagued by economic depression and one that now offered abundant opportunities. The 1944 "G.I. Bill" rewarded military service with the promise of government assistance in paying for technical training or higher education and low-interest loans to buy homes. As a result, millions of men (and some women) were able to attend college or learn a trade. The G.I. Bill was such a success that it remained a permanent program. Millions were also able to buy their own homes, which helped inspire a building boom that led to the development of suburbs all across America. Prosperity and home ownership also inspired another kind of boom—the baby boom. From 1946 to roughly 1964, the World War II generation had children in record numbers.

The years after World War II were tumultuous ones as well. The United States and Soviet Union emerged from the war as global superpowers, and even though they had been temporary allies during the war, their fundamentally different cultures and political philosophies quickly turned them into enemies during what was known as "the cold war." The new United Nations did provide a forum for negotiating global

The horrors of the Holocaust made the creation of a Jewish state a pressing concern after the war. These survivors of the Buchenwald concentration camp were relocated to Palestine, which became the nation of Israel in 1948. Unfortunately, religious and cultural differences in the Middle East have given Israel and the region a turbulent history since World War II.
National Archives, III-SC-207907

conflict, but at the core, the United States wanted to encourage capitalism and democracy, while the Soviet Union wanted communism to prevail. The postwar period became something of a political chess game as each nation tried to anticipate what the other would do. As a result, U.S. foreign policy for the next forty years became almost obsessed with containing communism in the countries where it already existed and preventing it from spreading like a cancer worldwide. Conventional wisdom held that if one country fell to communism, its neighbors would also fall like dominos. These ideas of "containment" and "the domino theory" led the United States to promote democracies through economic stability programs like the Marshall Plan and to intervene militarily in those nations threatening to become consumed by communism, such as Korea and Vietnam.

Events arising from World War II encouraged African Americans to test democracy at home. FDR's willingness to address racial discrimination in the defense industry, Truman's 1948 order to desegregate the military, and the loyal service of African Americans in the military all suggested that the times had changed enough to speed the course of racial progress. Through activism and legal means, the civil rights movement of the 1950s and 1960s broke down one racial barrier after another, even though prejudice still remained. The struggles of African Americans prompted other groups, such as women and American Indians, to fight for their own rights as well.

That the ideal of freedom fought for in World War II inspired later struggles makes an observation by Edward R. Murrow as true today as it was in his time: "Freedom is not to be bought in the bargain basement—nor for a lump sum—it must be paid for and argued about by each succeeding generation."[24]

Many of the leading Nazis who survived the war were put on trial at Nuremberg for assorted war crimes. The three men seated in the first row of the defendants' dock are, from left to right, Hermann Goering, Rudolf Hess, and Joachim von Ribbentrop. Each was found guilty, and Goering and von Ribbentrop were sentenced to hang, while Hess was sentenced to life in prison. National Archives, 238-NT-592

After years of economic depression in the 1930s, followed by wartime rationing, Americans finally had peace and prosperity. Thanks also to low-interest loans provided by the G.I. Bill, Americans bought their own homes in large numbers, prompting waves of tract-house development, like this one in Levittown, Pennsylvania, and the spread of suburbs across the nation. Library of Congress, LC-USZ62-127672, photograph courtesy of Hill & Knowlton, Inc.

NAVY NERVE CENTER
Wartime Expansion Has Brought Changes To Washington and the Navy Department

Opponents of the World War II Memorial argued that it would spoil the pristine vista from the Lincoln Memorial to the Washington Monument. While that view was unbroken in the late twentieth century, the site was far from pristine historically. During World War II, the Rainbow Pool site was ringed with ugly temporary office buildings used by the Navy (notice the walkways over the reflecting pool), which were not torn down until decades after the war. In some sense, it is appropriate that the World War II Memorial should now occupy what was once the wartime "Navy Nerve Center."[42] Bureau of Naval Personnel *Information Bulletin* (September 1944), Author's collection

CHAPTER TWO

CONSTRUCTING A MEMORIAL

At the end of the war, many veterans were more interested in getting on with their lives than in erecting monuments. Most memorials in the postwar period took a practical form, such as naming an auditorium for a local war hero. As the years passed, the country also became involved in other, more controversial wars, which soured many Americans on celebrating warfare.

Feelings changed over time, however. When World War II veteran Roger Durbin asked Ohio Congresswoman Marcy Kaptur why there was no World War II memorial in Washington, D.C., she replied that there was—the "Iwo Jima Memorial" near Arlington National Cemetery. Stunned to learn that this memorial honored only the Marine Corps, Kaptur (with Durbin's help) began a quest to make a World War II memorial in the nation's capital a reality. Although Kaptur introduced legislation in 1987, a bill establishing the memorial did not become law until 1993.[25]

Where to build the memorial was the next hurdle to overcome. Seven sites were originally proposed, and Constitution Gardens, between the Vietnam Veterans Memorial and 17th Street, gathered the most support until Charles Atherton of the U.S. Commission of Fine Arts suggested the Rainbow Pool along 17th Street.[26] This site ultimately fit the bill, and a ceremonial groundbreaking at the site was held in the fall of 1995.

The American Battle Monuments Commission (ABMC) asked the U.S.

Architect Friedrich St.Florian's 1997 winning design included high earth berms on the north and south sides and a sunken plaza several feet lower to accommodate the auditorium and exhibit space called for in the initial competition. When the requirement for these additional spaces was eliminated, St.Florian modified the memorial to its current dimensions. Courtesy of Friedrich St.Florian, AIA

General Services Administration in 1996 to open a competition for the design of the new memorial, with the winner being a design by architect Friedrich St.Florian. Austrian by birth, St.Florian spent much of his career on the faculty of the Rhode Island School of Design, while also earning international acclaim for both his theoretical work and completed architectural projects. St.Florian's design concept for the World War II Memorial offered a grand scale appropriate to the significance of the war, incorporated landscape elements, and joined a modern sensibility with a classical style common in earlier Washington architecture. The architectural style of the finished memorial evokes the "Art Deco classicism" popular in the 1930s and 1940s, both in the United States and in Europe. St.Florian's design also went beyond commemorating only the armed forces who served in the war to acknowledge the contributions made by Americans on the home front as well.[27]

In January 1997, President Bill Clinton announced the selection of St.Florian and his team of artists and architects, and the memorial appeared to be becoming a reality. The National World War II Memorial Campaign, co-chaired by Senator Robert Dole and Federal Express CEO Fred Smith, began fundraising for the project, appealing to corporate donors and the general public. Actor Tom Hanks, star of the 1998 film *Saving Private Ryan*, agreed to serve as a public spokesman to attract attention to the proposed memorial.

Yet, as has been the case for every tribute on the National Mall, the site and design aroused controversy. For the next few years, several groups, including the National Coalition to Save Our Mall, spearheaded efforts to block the memorial with a prolonged legal battle that ultimately reached the United States Supreme Court. Arguments against the memorial included its impact on the view from the Lincoln Memorial to the Washington Monument, the environmental effect of a large memorial built on a flood plain, concerns that the National Mall was in danger of becoming cluttered with monuments, and that the design too closely resembled fascist architecture of 1930s Germany. The Supreme Court denied the last petition in 2002.

With the legal obstacles removed, construction of the memorial got under way and was completed by 2004. The memorial was officially dedicated on May 29, 2004. Those who traveled to Washington for the dedication ceremony represented the last major gathering of the veterans of World War II. Most seemed pleased with the outcome of the memorial and only wished it had been completed sooner. "I look at this beautiful memorial and say it's long overdue," army veteran George Desiderio told the *Boston Globe* at the opening ceremonies. "I just wish some of my comrades who are gone now had seen it, because they would have appreciated it too."[28] Unfortunately, Roger Durbin, the veteran who inspired the memorial's creation, was not among the veterans at the dedication ceremonies. He passed away in 2000.

Saving Private Ryan star Tom Hanks addresses the audience at the official memorial dedication ceremony, May 29, 2004. Photo by Terry Adams/National Park Service

A crowd at the official dedication ceremony of the World War II Memorial, May 29, 2004. Photo by Terry Adams/National Park Service

Although just teenagers when America entered World War II,
Alexander and Ross Carter King epitomized wartime par-
ticipation on the homefront. He served with the Boy Scouts
on a Coast Guard cutter off Charleston, South Carolina, and rode his bicycle around Atlanta,
Georgia, as a civil defense messenger. She rolled bandages and was a nurses' aid for the Red
Cross. Standing in front of bas-reliefs at the World War II Memorial that celebrate events on
the home front, the Kings share their memories of the war with a park ranger at the memorial.
For this ranger the memorial evokes memories of his own parents. His mother volunteered
with the Red Cross at Mare Island Naval Hospital, while his father served on the USS Boise,
which saw action at Guadalcanal and supported American landings in Italy and Western
New Guinea. In the photo (inset), father and son participate in a V-E Day celebration at the
memorial in 2005. Author's collection, and courtesy of Michael Balis

Constitution Gardens Lake

Contemplative Area

Atlantic Pavilion

Atlantic Theater bas-reliefs

Atlantic Pavilion Plaza

Balustrades

Reflecting Pool

Freedom Wall

Rainbow Pool

Ceremonial Plaza

Ceremonial Entrance with Announcement Stone

17th Street

Pacific Pavilion Plaza

Pillars (56 surrounding plazas)

Pacific Pavilion

Pacific Theater bas-reliefs

Visitor Information Station

Home Front Dune

Restrooms

CHAPTER THREE

THE WORLD WAR II MEMORIAL

The World War II Memorial complex occupies a 7.4-acre site, of which 1.7 acres consists of the memorial itself. The map (on facing page) identifies the main elements of the memorial, and corresponds to the interpretive sections on the following pages.

Ceremonial Entrance

Visitors entering the memorial from 17th Street are greeted by an announcement stone, which places the memorial and the war it honors in the context of its location on the National Mall:

> HERE IN THE PRESENCE OF WASHINGTON AND LINCOLN, ONE THE EIGHTEENTH CENTURY FATHER AND THE OTHER THE NINETEENTH CENTURY PRESERVER OF OUR NATION, WE HONOR THOSE TWENTIETH CENTURY AMERICANS WHO TOOK UP THE STRUGGLE DURING THE SECOND WORLD WAR AND MADE THE SACRIFICES TO PERPETUATE THE GIFT OUR FOREFATHERS ENTRUSTED TO US: A NATION CONCEIVED IN LIBERTY AND JUSTICE.

Balustrade at ceremonial entrance. Author's collection

On each balustrade at the ceremonial entrance is the eagle from the Great Seal of the United States, each eagle turning its gaze inward toward the memorial. Such instances of balance can be found throughout the memorial, as the north and south sides appear as mirror images of one another. Above the eagles is the motto "E Pluribus Unum," Latin for "out of many, one," which in essence is what the memorial represents: the unity of the nation during the war.

To the north and south of the memorial's ceremonial entrance are flagpoles bearing on the base the names and emblems of the military forces that fought in World War II: Marine Corps, Army, Navy, Army Air Forces, Merchant Marine, and Coast Guard. On the granite bench under the flagpoles is inscribed the American mission during the war: AMERICANS CAME TO LIBERATE, NOT TO CONQUER, TO RESTORE FREEDOM AND TO END TYRANNY.

Design architect Friedrich St.Florian, inspired by the forums used in antiquity as places to gather, envisioned the World War II Memorial as a forum as well. The grass terraces leading from the ceremonial entrance to the plaza are used for public events.

These two British women help unload Winchester rifles that have just arrived in a lend-lease shipment from the United States. British Prime Minister Winston Churchill recognized that Allied access to seemingly inexhaustible American supplies in essence signed "Hitler's death warrant." America supplied nearly $50 billion in aid to its allies during the war.[44]
Library of Congress, LC-USZ62-90199

Bas-Reliefs

The balustrades of the ceremonial entrance feature twenty-four bronze bas-reliefs that celebrate the transformation of America during World War II. The twelve on the north wall largely pay homage to the country's participation in the Atlantic Theater, while the twelve on the south wall recognize aspects of the Pacific Theater.

For inspiration, sculptor Ray Kaskey consulted historical photographs from the era and dressed re-enactors in period clothing and accessories to re-create scenes in his studio. The resulting panels are visually appealing, and when taken together, tell the story of World War II from both the military and civilian perspective.

Lend-Lease/War Declared

War Bond Parade

The United States spent approximately $350 billion on the war. To help pay the bill, the government sold war stamps and bonds, and launched a public relations campaign encouraging Americans to invest. The posters, parades, and celebrity endorsements worked, prompting Americans to buy billions of dollars worth of bonds during the war. The public especially responded to posters reminding it of the human faces behind the war effort, which led to "an unprecedented print run" of 1.5 million "You buy 'em, we'll fly 'em!" posters.[45] Library of Congress, LC-USF34-072689-D; LC-USZC4-2751

Mobilization of Women

These nurses arrived in Scotland in 1944 to work in the European Theater. They were but a few of the almost 75,000 American military nurses who served during the war. Their jobs often brought them close to the front lines, and at least 250 female nurses lost their own lives while trying to save the lives of others.[46] In a segregated military, however, the nurses in this picture would only tend to black troops. National Archives, III-SC-192605-S

Men and Women at Work/Aircraft Construction

Women who worked in defense industries during the war were often referred to as "Rosie the Riveter," which was also the title of a 1942 song by Redd Evans and John Jacob Loeb that celebrated the dedication of Rosies everywhere. "All the day long whether rain or shine/She's a part of the assembly line/She's making history working for victory/Rosie…the riveter." (Want to sing along? Sheet music and lyrics may be found at http://www.rosietheriveter.org/rosiemusic.htm) Library of Congress, LC-DIG-fsac-1a35359

J. Howard Miller's ca. 1942 "We Can Do It!" poster for the War Production Coordinating Committee has become almost synonymous with "Rosie the Riveter" since the war and is now commonly seen on T-shirts and coffee mugs. National Archives, 179-WP-1563

Battle of the Atlantic

The Battle of the Atlantic went on throughout the war, as the Allies fought the Germans for control of the Atlantic and its vital transportation routes for supplies from America. Allied ships traveled in convoys for protection and dropped cylindrical depth charges (visible in the bas-relief) to disable the German submarines that prowled Atlantic waters. National Archives, 80-G-30979

Air War/B-17 Crew

Although this bas-relief celebrates the air and ground crews that kept the famous B-17 "Flying Fortresses" in the air, sculptor Ray Kaskey has also paid homage to the pets that many crewmen considered another "one of the guys." The pup in the relief had predecessors like "Flash," a little terrier who not only served as a mascot for his air wing but also went along on some of their flights. Soldiers on the ground frequently adopted pets as well, although Marines in the Pacific sometimes had to settle for more unusual native animals rather than the dogs and cats preferred by soldiers and seamen in the European Theater.[47] National Archives, 80-G-322697

Paratroopers

Since they might be on their own for several days after a drop, paratroopers needed to carry supplies and equipment for almost any situation. Thus, the average weight of a paratrooper's pack was seventy pounds, not including the parachute. That weight included a rifle, ammunition, compass, grenades, food rations and water (or water purification tablets), and any toiletries or personal effects.[48] National Archives, III-SC-354702

D-Day

This is what the men of the Sixteenth Infantry saw of Omaha Beach as they left their Coast Guard landing craft on D-Day (June 6, 1944). The D-Day invasion and similar amphibious landings in the Pacific would not have been possible without the landing craft seen here and in the bas-relief. The major manufacturer of these craft was Andrew Jackson Higgins, whose 36' by 10' LCVP boats were compared to a "floating cigar box." They were not comfortable, but they could land one platoon in a matter of minutes and immediately return to the transport ship for another. So vital were the twenty thousand "Higgins Boats" to military success that Eisenhower once remarked that Higgins "is the man who won the war for us."[49] National Archives, 26-G-2343

Tanks in Combat

Allied troops moving through occupied France had to contend with German snipers hiding in buildings and guns concealed behind the hedgerows that lined every country lane. While Allied soldiers appreciated the tanks for the firepower and cover they provided, "if you're a foot soldier you hate to be near a tank, for it always draws fire."[50] National Archives, III-SC-193903

Medics on Battlefield

Wounded soldiers like Private Roy Humphrey literally owed their lives to medics like Private First Class Harvey White for administering emergency first aid and blood products in the field that would sustain them until they could be taken to a medical facility. Many of the wounded also owed their lives to blood plasma, the collection and distribution of which was perfected as a result of the bloodletting of World War II. With the red blood cells removed, plasma did not have a blood "type" and could be used on anyone without fear of a negative reaction. Also, unlike whole blood, plasma could be stored for long periods of time (in a liquid, dried, or frozen state) until it was needed in the field. National Archives, III-SC-178198

Winter Combat/Battle of the Bulge

At the Battle of the Bulge (Dec. 1944–Jan. 1945), Allied troops fought the Germans and the severe winter weather, both of which were brutal and deadly. Progress was slow, and casualties due to battle wounds and frostbite were high. By the end of the campaign, sixteen thousand Americans were dead, another sixty thousand wounded or captured.[51] National Archives, III-SC-198534

Americans and Russians Meet at the Elbe River

American authorities agreed to let the Russians enter Berlin first in 1945, the honor of which cost the Russians about twenty thousand casualties. So it was that Russian forces welcomed the first Americans to cross the Elbe River in late April 1945. Although common interests allowed the Russians and Americans to cross broken bridges as allies during the war, the ideological battles between communism and capitalism would soon burn those bridges during the cold war that followed. National Archives, III-SC-205228

News of Pearl Harbor

Before there was television, before there was the Internet, there was radio. The vast majority of Americans received their news and entertainment over the radio, and it was through this medium that most Americans heard of the attack on Pearl Harbor on December 7, 1941. Radio had also helped sway American sympathy toward Britain in its fight against Germany in 1940, thanks largely to the reports of CBS radio reporter Edward R. Murrow (1908–1965), seen here at his broadcast desk. Murrow, one commentator remarked, had been heard "in the back kitchens and front living rooms and the moving automobiles and the hotdog stands of America."[52] National Archives, 80-G-45774

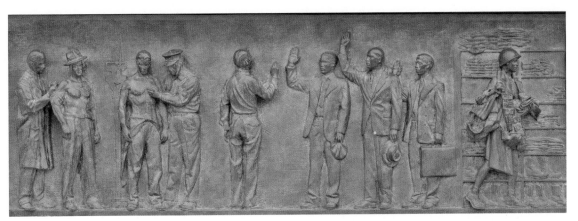

Draft Physical/Swearing In/Equipment Issue

Men entered enlistment centers as civilians but walked out as G.I.'s,
or "government issue," if they were Army men. Other branches of the
military used different "terms of endearment" for their inductees.
Library of Congress, LC-USW33-026129-C

Embarkation of Men

The accommodations were not luxurious on transport ships, as these soldiers on the SS Pennant discovered. To maximize sleeping space at night and elbow room during the day, men were assigned metal-and-canvas "racks" that folded up when not in use. National Archives, III-SC-172004

West Coast Shipbuilding

If Rosie the Riveter worked in aircraft construction, her counterpart in the shipyards could have been Wendy the Welder, welding being one of the secrets to the quick construction of Liberty ships. Here, a group of women prepare to weld their first piece of the SS George Washington Carver *at the Kaiser Shipyards in Richmond, California, ca. 1943.* National Archives, 208-NP-1HHH-5

Agriculture

As this poster suggests, men who worked in agriculture were often given draft exemptions because their work was considered vital to feeding the armies. Roughly twenty million Americans planted their own "victory gardens" to supplement the produce available on the home front.[53] National Archives, 44-PA-2112

Submarine Warfare

German U-boats received much attention for their attacks on Allied shipping early in the war, but American submarines were equally effective in torpedoing Japanese merchant ships, thereby helping to cut off supplies to the island nation. National Archives, 226-FPL-4-13

Navy Fighter Planes on Deck

Aircraft carriers during World War II forever changed naval warfare. Planes launched from carriers could attack targets on land, hit enemy ships below or engage their aircraft over the sea, and provide air cover for amphibious landings. National Archives, 80-G-204747A

Amphibious Landing

Successful amphibious landings required so much cooperation between air, ground, and naval forces that Winston Churchill called it "triphibious warfare," and the U.S. Marines were particularly skilled at it by the end of the war.[54] National Archives, 26-G-4718

Jungle Warfare

Advertisements during the war often used military imagery to sell products, like this ad for Fleet's Chap Stick, which appeared in Look *magazine in 1943. One can only imagine how the tough Marines in this photograph would have felt knowing they were being accused of wearing "lipstick"!* Author's collection

Tough—but they use lipstick

U. S. Navy Photo from International

A fighting man's lips can get into a lot of trouble if they aren't cared for—so can yours. Dust, dirt, wind, sun, heat, and cold can cause painful lip troubles. That's why many soldiers use a special lip protective—Fleet's Chap Stick —the biggest little thing in the soldier's pack. Avoid unsightly lip conditions that may become serious by making lip care a daily habit—your own doctor will tell you it's a *good* one! Use

Fleet's Chap Stick. Gently medicated, it is made especially for the lips—gives lips a "film of protection." Soothes and helps heal chapped and wind-burned lips, too. Get a handy "vest pocket" Chap Stick today. Only 25¢. On sale at drug counters, PX's and Ship's Service Stores everywhere. And ON DUTY WITH U.S. FIGHTING MEN THE WORLD OVER. Chap Stick Co., Lynchburg, Va.

Guard *Chap Stick* **your lips...** morning— noon— and night

Field Burial

"On Guadalcanal many boys are not yet buried in that cemetery and perhaps never will be," First Lady Eleanor Roosevelt observed. *"They were buried when the fighting was on and where they fell. The grave was marked, but then the fight had to go forward. Wherever they lie, however, is consecrated ground since they gave their lives so others might live in peace and freedom."*[55] National Archives, 26-G-2441

Liberation of POWs

Some of the Allied soldiers who survived the Bataan Death March in 1942 also survived years of abuse and starvation at the hands of their Japanese captors. The average POW in the Pacific lost thirty-eight pounds during his captivity.[56] When the Philippines were liberated in 1945, so were the emaciated survivors of Bataan. National Archives, III-SC-334296

V-J Day

Both V-E (Victory in Europe) and V-J (Victory in Japan) Days prompted dancing in the streets and other wild celebrations. This Italian neighborhood in New York erupted with joy at the announcement of Japan's surrender. National Archives, 80-G-377094

The oculus above the baldachinos in the pavilions provides additional light and transparency to the heaviness of the granite structure and also provides an inspiring view skyward.

This World War II Victory Medal was earned by George B. Howe for his wartime service. Howe began his naval career on the USS Constitution *in 1932, survived the bombing at Pearl Harbor, and went on to earn the rank of captain in the United States Navy before retiring in 1972. Medal and photo courtesy of Linda H. Cunningham*

Pavilions

Two forty-three-foot-tall granite pavilions, honoring the Atlantic and Pacific theaters of war, anchor the north and south sides of the memorial's plaza. Within each pavilion are bronze baldachinos that form a canopy of four bald eagles holding aloft a laurel wreath. All these elements are symbolic in that the bald eagle is the national bird, laurel wreaths signify victory, and baldachinos can be canopies over church altars—together representing a sort of civic religion of shared history during the war.

Embedded in the floor of each pavilion is a replica of the World War II Victory Medal that was awarded to all who served on active duty in the American armed forces between December 7, 1941, and December 31, 1946. In the medal, the female form of "Liberation" steps victoriously on a war helmet while holding pieces of a broken sword in her hands. The sun rises in the background, indicating the dawn of peace.

Surrounding the victory medal are the phrases "Victory on Land," "Victory at Sea," and "Victory in the Air," as well as the years of America's involvement in the war, 1941–1945. Visitors entering the Atlantic pavilion from the north will first see "Victory on Land," acknowledging that campaigns in the Atlantic Theater were largely fought on land. Likewise, visitors entering the Pacific pavilion from the south will be met

Victory Medal replica in pavilion floor.

with "Victory at Sea," recognizing the naval character of the Pacific Theater.

Below each pavilion, in the fountains facing the plaza, are inscribed four theaters of operation. Inscribed along the rim of the basin are the names or locations of individual campaigns crucial to achieving victory in that respective theater of war. The campaigns are listed in roughly chronological order, from left to right. The Atlantic Theater begins with an inscription for the Battle of the Atlantic and ends where the European war ended, Germany. The Pacific Theater opens with Pearl Harbor and ends with the occupation of Japan.

It is beyond the scope of this book to describe each of the individual campaigns inscribed on the memorial, but visitors may best understand them as elements of a large puzzle in which one piece had to be fitted before the next could be locked into place.

Why were these men from the 313th Infantry smiling in June 1945? Because the European war had ended, and they had survived it. As did so many other soldiers, Fred Cerra (kneeling, far left) returned home to Kansas City, Missouri, after the war, married his sweetheart down the block, and immediately began a family. He spent much of his postwar career working for General Motors before retiring in 1983. This "everyman soldier" lived a full life before passing away in 1992. Courtesy of Marilyn Waterhouse

Just like their comrades in the Atlantic Theater, there was always time for a group photo. These Marine raiders pose in the midst of jungle warfare on Bougainville in the Solomon Islands in January 1944. National Archives, 80-G-205686

Atlantic pavilion. Author's collection

Atlantic Theater

NORTH AFRICA ★ SOUTHERN EUROPE ★ WESTERN EUROPE ★ CENTRAL EUROPE

BATTLE OF THE ATLANTIC ★ MURMANSK RUN ★ TUNISIA ★ SICILY SALERNO ANZIO ROME PO VALLEY ★ NORMANDY ★ ST. LÔ ★ AIR WAR IN EUROPE ★ ALSACE ★ RHINELAND ★ HUERTGEN FOREST ★ BATTLE OF THE BULGE ★ REMAGEN BRIDGE ★ GERMANY

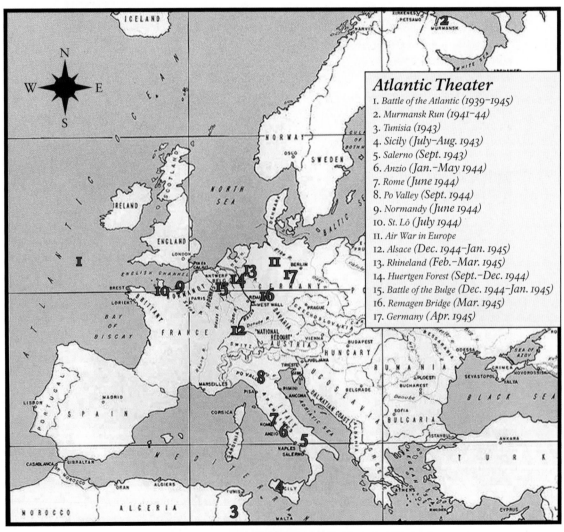

Atlantic Theater

1. *Battle of the Atlantic (1939–1945)*
2. *Murmansk Run (1941–44)*
3. *Tunisia (1943)*
4. *Sicily (July–Aug. 1943)*
5. *Salerno (Sept. 1943)*
6. *Anzio (Jan.–May 1944)*
7. *Rome (June 1944)*
8. *Po Valley (Sept. 1944)*
9. *Normandy (June 1944)*
10. *St. Lô (July 1944)*
11. *Air War in Europe*
12. *Alsace (Dec. 1944–Jan. 1945)*
13. *Rhineland (Feb.–Mar. 1945)*
14. *Huertgen Forest (Sept.–Dec. 1944)*
15. *Battle of the Bulge (Dec. 1944–Jan. 1945)*
16. *Remagen Bridge (Mar. 1945)*
17. *Germany (Apr. 1945)*

Geography and Coalitions, Europe and the Middle East. Map courtesy of the Department of History, United States Military Academy

Pacific Theater

CHINA-BURMA-INDIA ★ SOUTHWEST PACIFIC ★ CENTRAL PACIFIC
★ NORTH PACIFIC

PEARL HARBOR ★ WAKE ISLAND ★ BATAAN CORREGIDOR ★
CORAL SEA ★ MIDWAY ★ GUADALCANAL ★ NEW GUINEA ★ BUNA
★ TARAWA ★ KWAJALEIN ★ ATTU ★ SAIPAN TINIAN GUAM ★
PHILIPPINE SEA ★ PELELIU ★ LEYTE GULF ★ LUZON ★ MANILA ★
IWO JIMA ★ OKINAWA ★ JAPAN

Pacific pavilion. Author's collection

Pacific Theater

1. *Pearl Harbor (Dec. 7, 1941)*
2. *Wake Island (Dec. 1941)*
3. *Bataan (1941–April 1942)*
4. *Corregidor (Dec. 1941–May 1942; Feb. 1945)*
5. *Coral Sea (May 1942)*
6. *Midway (June 1942)*
7. *Guadalcanal (Aug. 1942–Feb. 1943)*
8. *New Guinea (July–Sept. 1942; first campaign)*
9. *Buna (Jan. 1943)*
10. *Tarawa (Nov. 1943)*
11. *Kwajalein (Feb. 1944)*
12. *Attu (May 1943)*
13. *Saipan (June–July 1944)*
14. *Tinian (Aug. 1944)*
15. *Guam (Aug. 1944)*
16. *Philippine Sea (June 1944)*
17. *Peleliu (Sept.–Oct. 1944)*
18. *Leyte Gulf (Oct. 1944)*
19. *Luzon (Jan. 1945)*
20. *Manila (Feb.–Mar. 1945)*
21. *Iwo Jima (Feb.–Mar. 1945)*
22. *Okinawa (Apr.–Jun. 1945)*
23. *Japan (1945)*

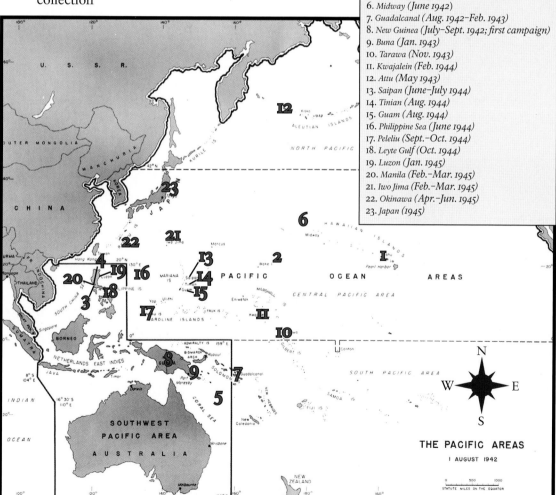

Pacific Areas, 1 August 1942. From American Military History, United States Army Center of Military History, 1989

Inscriptions

At each end of the colonnades and below the pavilion balconies are excerpts of statements by notable Americans of World War II about aspects of the war and those who served. The quotations facing the plaza itself are placed chronologically from east to west, with President Roosevelt beginning the sequence in the east to President Truman ending it in the west.

Atlantic Pavilion Plaza

Library of Congress,
LC-USZ62-122229

WOMEN WHO STEPPED UP WERE MEASURED AS CITIZENS OF THE NATION, NOT AS WOMEN...THIS WAS A PEOPLE'S WAR, AND EVERYONE WAS IN IT.

PEOPLE'S WAR, AND EVERYONE WAS IN IT.

COLONEL OVETA CULP HOBBY

Like many women of her day, Oveta Culp Hobby's (1905–1995) life changed when she married, in her case to a former governor of Texas. But Hobby excelled in her own right as a civic leader, businesswoman, and, during World War II, as the director of the pioneering Women's Army Corps. She became the first secretary of the Department of Health, Education, and Welfare in 1953, and served on numerous charitable boards and commissions throughout her long life.

Library of Congress,
LC-USZ62-90270

THEY HAVE GIVEN THEIR SONS TO THE MILITARY SERVICES. THEY HAVE STOKED THE FURNACES AND HURRIED THE FACTORY WHEELS. THEY HAVE MADE THE PLANES AND WELDED THE TANKS, RIVETED THE SHIPS AND ROLLED THE SHELLS.

PRESIDENT FRANKLIN D. ROOSEVELT

Before the Twenty-second Amendment limited presidents to two terms, Franklin D. Roosevelt (1882–1945) served longer than any other president, from 1933 to 1945. He guided the nation through the depths of the Great Depression and the tragedy and triumph of the Second World War. In this 1942 Labor Day address, Roosevelt acknowledged the contribution of America's work force to the war effort.

Library of Congress, LC-USZ62-86845

D-DAY JUNE 6, 1944

YOU ARE ABOUT TO EMBARK UPON THE GREAT CRUSADE TOWARD WHICH WE HAVE STRIVEN THESE MANY MONTHS. THE EYES OF THE WORLD ARE UPON YOU...I HAVE FULL CONFIDENCE IN YOUR COURAGE, DEVOTION TO DUTY AND SKILL IN BATTLE.

GENERAL DWIGHT D. EISENHOWER

Dwight D. Eisenhower (1890–1969) gained fame during World War II by leading the American invasion forces in North Africa and Italy in 1943 and by his appointment as supreme commander of the Allied forces in Europe, which put him in charge of the D-Day invasion in 1944. The inscription above is an excerpt from his inspirational June 6 order of the day to the troops. Eisenhower's postwar popularity propelled him to the presidency in 1952, and he served two terms as the commander-in-chief.

Library of Congress, LC-USZ62-61397

WE ARE DETERMINED THAT BEFORE THE SUN SETS ON THIS TERRIBLE STRUGGLE OUR FLAG WILL BE RECOGNIZED THROUGHOUT THE WORLD AS A SYMBOL OF FREEDOM ON THE ONE HAND AND OF OVERWHELMING FORCE ON THE OTHER.

GENERAL GEORGE C. MARSHALL

George C. Marshall (1880–1959) served as chief of staff of the army during World War II, and his military skill and calm personality led Winston Churchill to call him "the true organizer of victory."[29] *After the war, Marshall helped ensure that the American flag would represent freedom and power by serving as secretary of state and secretary of defense under President Truman, and he proposed the "Marshall Plan" that provided economic aid to rebuild war-torn countries in Europe.*

National Archives, 44-PA-2218

THE HEROISM OF OUR OWN TROOPS...WAS MATCHED BY THAT OF THE ARMED FORCES OF THE NATIONS THAT FOUGHT BY OUR SIDE...THEY ABSORBED THE BLOWS...AND THEY SHARED TO THE FULL IN THE ULTIMATE DESTRUCTION OF THE ENEMY.

PRESIDENT HARRY S TRUMAN

This 1943 poster issued by the Office of War Information suggests the same sentiment that President Harry Truman would later express regarding the significance of America's allies in winning World War II. In the foreground, cannons displaying the flags of the "Big Three" nations of Great Britain, the United States, and the Soviet Union are joined by the cannons of other allied nations, symbolizing the unity that led to victory for the Allies.

Pacific Pavilion Plaza

THEY FOUGHT TOGETHER AS BROTHERS-IN-ARMS. THEY DIED TOGETHER AND NOW THEY SLEEP SIDE BY SIDE. TO THEM WE HAVE A SOLEMN OBLIGATION.

ADMIRAL CHESTER W. NIMITZ

Chester W. Nimitz (1885–1966) commanded the Navy's Pacific Fleet during World War II, supervising the campaigns that led to the destruction of Japan's naval forces. Nimitz was one of the American representatives who signed Japan's surrender document ending the war, and it was this occasion that prompted his reflection on the debt of the living to the sacrifices of the dead. Nimitz served as chief of naval operations after the war.

U.S. Naval Historical Center, NH 85044

PEARL HARBOR

DECEMBER 7, 1941, A DATE WHICH WILL LIVE IN INFAMY...NO MATTER HOW LONG IT MAY TAKE US TO OVERCOME THIS PREMEDITATED INVASION, THE AMERICAN PEOPLE, IN THEIR RIGHTEOUS MIGHT, WILL WIN THROUGH TO ABSOLUTE VICTORY.

PRESIDENT FRANKLIN D. ROOSEVELT

Roosevelt appeared before a joint session of Congress on December 8, 1941, to ask for a declaration of war against Japan. The quote above is an excerpt from his address to Congress and, via radio, to the entire nation. The sentence ending in "absolute victory" earned Roosevelt the most thunderous and sustained applause of the speech by his audience in Congress. Later in this speech, Roosevelt expressed confidence in the American people and its military to "gain the inevitable triumph–so help us God."[30] Here President Roosevelt signs the declaration of war approved by Congress.

Library of Congress, LC-USZ62-128756

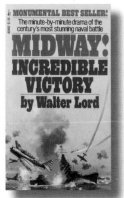

Book cover from Incredible Victory *by Walter Lord, copyright © 1967 by Walter Lord. Reprinted by permission of HarperCollins Publishers.* Book courtesy of Susan Reyburn.

BATTLE OF MIDWAY, JUNE 4–7, 1942

THEY HAD NO RIGHT TO WIN. YET THEY DID, AND IN DOING SO THEY CHANGED THE COURSE OF A WAR...EVEN AGAINST THE GREATEST OF ODDS, THERE IS SOMETHING IN THE HUMAN SPIRIT—A MAGIC BLEND OF SKILL, FAITH AND VALOR—THAT CAN LIFT MEN FROM CERTAIN DEFEAT TO INCREDIBLE VICTORY.

WALTER LORD, AUTHOR

Although many know Walter Lord (1917–2002) as the author of books on the famous luxury liner Titanic, *which struck an iceberg and sank on its maiden voyage in 1912, he also wrote important volumes about World War II, including* Incredible Victory *(1967) on the battle of Midway, quoted above. Lord worked during the war for the Office of Strategic Services, predecessor of the Central Intelligence Agency (CIA).*

National Archives, 26-G-3584

THE WAR'S END

TODAY THE GUNS ARE SILENT. A GREAT TRAGEDY HAS ENDED. A GREAT VICTORY HAS BEEN WON. THE SKIES NO LONGER RAIN DEATH—THE SEAS BEAR ONLY COMMERCE—MEN EVERYWHERE WALK UPRIGHT IN THE SUNLIGHT. THE ENTIRE WORLD IS QUIETLY AT PEACE.

GENERAL DOUGLAS MACARTHUR

Douglas MacArthur (1880–1964) was serving as commander of army forces in the Far East when the Japanese attacked American bases in the Pacific in December 1941. After vowing to return to the Philippines, he headed the liberation forces that landed on the archipelago in 1945. After accepting the Japanese surrender document on September 2, 1945, MacArthur guided the American occupation of Japan (1945–1950) and served as supreme allied commander of United Nations forces in Korea until recalled by President Truman in 1951.

Library of Congress, LC-USZ62- 98170

OUR DEBT TO THE HEROIC MEN AND VALIANT WOMEN IN THE SERVICE OF OUR COUNTRY CAN NEVER BE REPAID. THEY HAVE EARNED OUR UNDYING GRATITUDE. AMERICA WILL NEVER FORGET THEIR SACRIFICES.

PRESIDENT HARRY S TRUMAN

A veteran of World War I, Harry S Truman (1884–1972) understood the sacrifices made by a people at war. Truman was a United States senator from Missouri when he was tapped to be President Roosevelt's running mate in 1944 but became president himself when Roosevelt died just months into his fourth term. Truman guided the nation through the last months of World War II and through most of the conflict in Korea from 1950 to 1953.

Freedom Wall

Freedom Wall

A tradition began during World War I in which families hung in their front window a banner indicating with blue stars how many servicemen that household had given to the war effort. If one of those servicemen was killed in the line of duty, his blue star was covered with a gold star to indicate that the serviceman and his family had made the ultimate sacrifice. This practice was continued in World War II. The gold star, then, came to symbolize the individual cost of freedom.

The Freedom Wall at the western side of the memorial incorporates the gold star motif to explain the phrase inscribed at the edge of the reflecting pool: HERE WE MARK THE PRICE OF FREEDOM. Attached to the Freedom Wall is a field of 4,048 gold stars, with each star representing 100 Americans who died or remain missing in the war, a total of more than 400,000 lives lost.

One of those lost lives belonged to Private Francis Vishnosky (1922–1944) of the Seventh Field Artillery Battalion. Private Vishnosky enlisted in the army at the age of eighteen, mostly out of necessity after his mother died and his older siblings all established their own homes. He survived campaigns in North Africa and Sicily, and even the first wave of landings on D-Day, which he described to his sister, Mary Schmitzer, as "pretty hot . . . and I don't mean the weather." Two weeks later, too tired to dig a foxhole after a day on the front lines, Private Vishnosky pitched a pup tent and was fatally wounded on June 23, 1944, by German artillery rounds that pierced the tent. Like many other Americans, Vishnosky's sister received a telegram from the War Department regretfully announcing the death of a loved one.

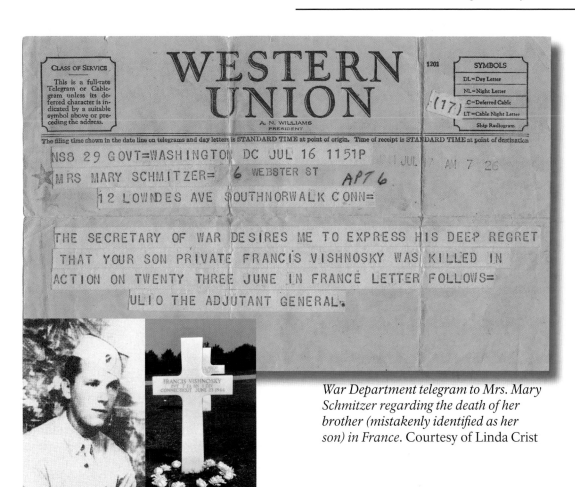

War Department telegram to Mrs. Mary Schmitzer regarding the death of her brother (mistakenly identified as her son) in France. Courtesy of Linda Crist

Private Francis Vishnosky in uniform and his grave in the Normandy American Cemetery in France.

The Freedom Wall is one of the few places in the memorial designed to direct the visitor's attention toward that element alone. While the roaring waterfalls on either side of the wall have the effect of silencing background noise, some visitors seem to hear in the rhythmic falling of the water the sound of drums beating as if at a funeral procession.

The symbolism of the gold star banner was incorporated into a popular wartime poster suggesting that silence could literally be a matter of life or death if crucial intelligence fell into enemy hands. Library of Congress, LC-USZC4-2749

Pillars

The fifty-six pillars surrounding the plaza each bear the name of a state, territory, or district under the authority of the United States during World War II. The pillars are arranged chronologically by their entrance date into the federal union or acquisition by the United States but alternate from south to north of the Freedom Wall. Delaware was the first state to enter the union, and it is the first pillar to the left of the Freedom Wall. The second state, Pennsylvania, is located to the right of the wall. The remaining states follow this left-to-right pattern around the plaza, with the District of Columbia and territories at the end of the chain.

Each seventeen-foot pillar is exactly alike, except for the name of the state or territory. This uniformity signifies that each state or territory played a vital role in the overall war effort, and none should be counted as more important than any other. The open space within each pillar not only adds light and transparency to the memorial design but can also be interpreted as representing what each state and territory lost in residents who gave their lives for the war effort. Extending the metaphor of unity among the states and territories, each pillar is connected to its neighbor with a segment of bronze rope, indicating that the entire country literally was bound together by the common experience of war.

Each pillar also supports two wreaths, the patterns of which alternate from pillar to pillar on the front and back. The wreath of oak leaves symbolizes the military and industrial might of the United States, while the wheat wreath represents the agricultural strength that sustained American troops and their allies during the war.

Wheat wreath. Author's photo

Oak wreath. Author's photo

Rainbow Pool

The Rainbow Pool, with Atlantic pavilion and state pillars in the background.

The Rainbow Pool at the memorial echoes—but is 15 percent smaller than—the pool constructed in the 1920s that once occupied this site. It is also six feet lower than the land surrounding the memorial, which allows the fountains to reach their full capacity without obstructing the view between the Washington Monument and Lincoln Memorial. The fountains may not be at their highest at any given time, however, because they are equipped with sensors that detect changes in wind and weather conditions. A sustained gust of wind, for example, will prompt the fountain to reduce the height of its spray to keep the falling water within the confines of the pool, rather than on visitors downwind. Regardless of the velocity of the water, the fountains in the Rainbow Pool, and indeed the water features throughout the memorial, have the effect of not only symbolizing the bodies of water over which the Second World War was fought but also of drowning out much of the noise from busy streets nearby and air traffic above.

The coloring of the Brazilian Rio Verde and Moss Green granite stones in the plaza surrounding the pool is also intended to soften the memorial. The shades of green give variety to the expanse of gray granite elsewhere in the plaza, pick up the green tones of the bronze features, and feel like an extension of the lawn on the slope leading down to the pool and the green spaces on the National Mall beyond the memorial.[31]

Even the memorial's water drainage grates have a symbolic design. The star within a circle, flanked by two heavy lines, evokes the insignia painted on American aircraft, like the one shown here on a SB2C plane coming in for a landing on an aircraft carrier.
National Archives, 80-G-376123

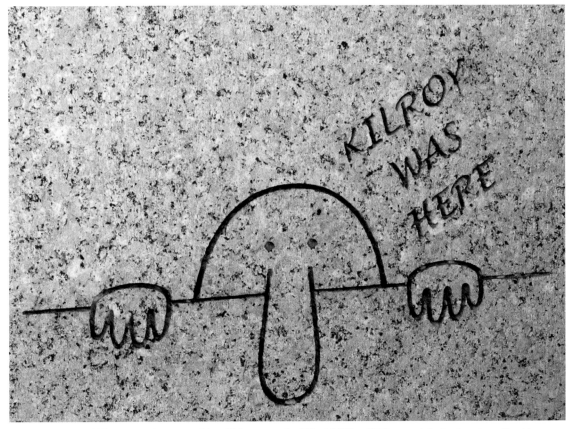

Kilroy was here, and is still here on the World War II Memorial. Author's collection

Kilroy

Those with keen eyesight may have already spotted the Kilroys on each side of the service entrances behind the Freedom Wall on the upper level. The comical drawing of the little man with the big nose and the phrase "KILROY WAS HERE" was graffiti left by Americans in their military travels around the world. Assorted legends claim that there was a real Kilroy, including a welding inspector named James J. Kilroy who chalked "Kilroy was here" on inspected materials. By the end of the war, Kilroy had indeed been "here" everywhere and was a beloved figure to American servicemen. So beloved, that workers on the World War II memorial had Kilroy etched into the memorial without telling anyone! When Kilroy was discovered, everyone agreed that his presence was very appropriate, and now veterans visiting the memorial often ask to be taken to see Kilroy once more.

World War II Honoree

Civilian on the Home Front

Harry C. Waterhouse

HOMETOWN
San Diego, CA

HONORED BY
Miss Michelle A. Krowl

ACTIVITY DURING WWII
BLOCK CAPTAIN FOR MISSION BEACH (SAN DIEGO) CIVILIAN DEFENSE
PATROL, AND WELDER ON MILITARY AIRCRAFT PRODUCED AT SOLAR
AIRCRAFT COMPANY.

Sample entry from the World War II Memorial online registry. Author's collection

Visitors Information Station

An information station for visitors is located just south of the Pacific pavilion. There, National Park Service representatives answer questions, distribute brochures, and meet visitors for guided tours of the memorial. Four touch-screen computers at the station give visitors access to the World War II Registry, an online list of individuals who contributed to the war effort, either in the military or on the home front. The registry is also available at http://www.wwiimemorial.com. Veterans interested in sharing their war stories may also want to contact the Veterans History Project at the Library of Congress, www.loc.gov/vets.

Contemplative Area

Visitors who need to escape the crowds for a moment of quiet reflection may want to visit the contemplative area, located just north of the Atlantic pavilion. The circular area provides benches on which to rest and a soothing landscape that echoes the green and white colors of the memorial landscape itself.

NATIONAL PARK SERVICE SITES OF RELEVANCE TO WORLD WAR II EVENTS AND PERSONALITIES

(visit www.nps.gov to find out more about the individual sites)

Alabama
Tuskegee Airmen National Historic Site (Tuskegee)

Alaska
Aleutian World War II National Historical Park (Aleutian Islands)

California
Golden Gate National Recreation Area (San Francisco Bay Area)
Manzanar National Historic Site (Owens Valley, near Independence, CA)
Port Chicago Naval Magazine National Memorial (Concord)
Rosie the Riveter/WWII Home Front National Historical Park (Richmond)

District of Columbia
Edward R. Murrow Park (Pennsylvania Avenue, at 18th Street, NW)
First Division Monument (17th and E Streets, NW, near the White House)
Franklin Delano Roosevelt Memorial (West Potomac Park)
National Memorial to Japanese American Patriotism in World War II (Louisiana and New Jersey Avenues, at D Street, NW)
Second Division Memorial (Constitution Avenue, near 17th Street, NW)

Guam
War in the Pacific National Historical Park (Piti, Guam)

Hawaii
USS Arizona Memorial (Honolulu)

Maine
Roosevelt Campobello International Park (Campobello Island)

Missouri
Harry S Truman National Historic Site (Independence)

New York
Eleanor Roosevelt National Historic Site (Hyde Park)
Home of Franklin D. Roosevelt National Historic Site (Hyde Park)

Northern Mariana Islands
American Memorial Park (Saipan)

Pennsylvania
Eisenhower National Historic Site (Gettysburg)

Virginia
George Washington Memorial Parkway (Arlington segment)
    Memorial Drive monuments (including the Seabees, 101st Airborne Division Memorial)
    Netherlands Carillon
    United States Marine Corps War Memorial (a.k.a. "Iwo Jima Memorial")
    Women in Military Service for America Memorial

A view from the Washington Monument of the World War II Memorial at dusk.

FOR FURTHER READING

The literature on World War II–related topics is vast and grows larger by the day. The following list only suggests works that present overviews of the war and are a starting place for readers eager to learn more about the war in general before branching out into more specialized subjects.

Churchill, Winston. *Memoirs of the Second World War.* Boston, 1990 (reprint).

Dear, I. C. B., ed. *The Oxford Companion to World War II.* New York, 2001.

Gilbert, Martin. *The Second World War: A Complete History.* Rev. ed. New York, 1991.

Goodwin, Doris Kearns. *No Ordinary Time: Franklin & Eleanor Roosevelt: The Home Front in World War II.* New York, 1994.

Keegan, John. *The Second World War.* New York, 1990.

Kennedy, David. *Freedom from Fear: The American People in Depression and War, 1929–1945.* New York, 1999.

Messenger, Charles. *The Chronological Atlas of World War Two.* New York, n.d.

Nichols, David, ed. *Ernie's War: The Best of Ernie Pyle's World War II Dispatches.* New York, 1986.

Sulzberger, C. L. *American Heritage New History of World War II.* Revised and updated by Stephen E. Ambrose. New York, 1997.

Terkel, Studs. *The "Good War": An Oral History of World War Two.* New York, 1984.

Time-Life Books. *WWII: The Illustrated History of World War II.* Alexandria, Va., 1999.

★★★★
ACKNOWLEDGMENTS

My thanks to Dennis Walton and Pamela Koch of Donning Publishers, Karen Cucurullo and Lance Hatten of the National Park Service, and Stacy Madalena of Eastern National for bringing me on board and providing guidance throughout this project. Park rangers are invaluable sources of advice and inspiration for interpreting memorials, and for their comments and suggestions, I thank Lowell Fry, Harry Hagen, Carol Kelly, David Rappel, and especially Michael Balis, Brad Berger, and Michael Kelly. Carol Highsmith's excellent photography brings the memorial to life. Historians Caroline Cox and Susan Reyburn cheerfully consulted on World War II topics and my text. For ransacking family archives to provide visuals for this book, George and Kathleen Krowl, Linda Cunningham, Linda Crist, Robert and Marilyn Waterhouse, and Larry and Sharon Beeman have my eternal gratitude. Bradley Gernand blazed the trail for this project and generally makes my life more interesting. But most of all, to the men and women of what have become known as the "Greatest Generation," we all owe a debt for their sacrifices, whether large or small, made in the fight for freedom, both at home and abroad.

Next Page: *Pacific pavilion at the World War II Memorial*

NOTES

Note to reader: Only sources providing direct quotations or specific data not considered common knowledge are included in the endnotes.

1. Leon F. Litwack and Winthrop D. Jordan, *The United States: Becoming a World Power, Volume II*, 7th ed. (Englewood Cliffs, N.J., 1991), p. 695.

2. Philip Morrison, quoted in Studs Terkel, *The "Good War": An Oral History of World War Two* (New York, 1984), p. 516.

3. Winston Churchill, quoted in Doris Kearns Goodwin, *No Ordinary Time: Franklin and Eleanor Roosevelt: The Home Front in World War II* (New York, 1994), p. 290; Carlo D'Este, "Victory in Europe," in Douglas Brinkley, ed. *The World War II Memorial: A Grateful Nation Remembers* (Washington, D.C., 2004), p. 79.

4. Litwack and Jordan, p. 710; Emily Yellin, *Our Mothers' War: American Women at Home and at the Front during World War II* (New York, 2004), pp. 57, 61; David M. Kennedy, *Freedom from Fear: The American People in Depression and War, 1929–1945* (New York, 1999), pp. 652, 654.

5. C. L. Sulzberger, *American Heritage New History of World War II*, revised and updated by Stephen E. Ambrose (New York, 1997), pp. 226–27.

6. Kennedy, *Freedom from Fear*, pp. 710–12.

7. Franklin D. Roosevelt, quoted in Yellin, *Our Mothers' War*, p. 39.

8. Quoted in Litwack and Jordan, *The United States*, p. 711; Yellin, *Our Mothers' War*, p. 47.

9. Yellin, *Our Mothers' War*, p. 207.

10. "Ex-Pilot Confirms Bomber Loss," *Washington Post*, December 17, 2006. It was thought that the Tuskegee Airmen had not lost a single bomber to enemy fire until historians of the Tuskegee Airmen announced in 2006 that official records proved otherwise. Even with this correction, the Airmen amassed an exemplary record of successful bomber escort missions.

11. *The Tuskegee Airmen*, produced and directed by W. Drew Perkins and Bill Reifenberger, Rubicon Productions (Alexandria, Va.: PBS Home Video, 2003); Biographical information on Benjamin O. Davis Jr., Arlington National Cemetery Website, http://www.arlingtoncemetery.net/bodavisjr.htm (accessed July 2006).

12. "This Month in History," *Smithsonian* (April 2005), p. 50; column for September 19, 1942, in Eleanor Roosevelt, *Eleanor Roosevelt's My Day: Her Acclaimed Columns, 1936–1945*, ed. Rochelle Chadakoff (New York, 1989), p. 255.

13. "A More Perfect Union: Japanese Americans & the Constitution," online exhibit by the National Museum of American History, Smithsonian Institution, http://americanhistory.si.edu/perfectunion/experience/index.html (accessed June 2006); David K. Fremon, *Japanese-American Internment in American History* (Springfield, N.J., 1996).

14. Thomas Childers, "Victory in the Air," in Brinkley, ed., *The World War II Memorial*, pp. 190, 197.

15. Harry Parley, quoted in Stephen E. Ambrose, *D-Day, June 6, 1944: The Climactic Battle of World War II* (New York, 1994), p. 335.

16. Kennedy, *Freedom from Fear*, p. 741.

17. William Casey, quoted in Peter Novick, *The Holocaust in American Life* (Boston and New York, 1999), p. 24.

18. "America and the Holocaust," *American Experience* series, PBS, online transcript available at http://www.pbs.org/wgbh/amex/holocaust (accessed May 2006); Novick, *The Holocaust in American Life*, pp. 19–59; Goodwin, *No Ordinary Time*, pp. 396–97.

19. Dwight D. Eisenhower, quoted in Ronald Takaki, *Double Victory: A Multicultural History of America in World War II* (Boston, 2000), p. 212.

20. Kennedy, *Freedom from Fear*, p. 530.

21. Michael J. Lyons, *World War II: A Short History* (Englewood Cliffs, N.J., 1989), p. 180.

22. Lyons, *World War II*, p. 303.

23. Dellie Hahne, quoted in Mark Jonathan Harris, Franklin Mitchell, and Steven Schechter, eds., *The Homefront: America During World War II* (New York, 1984), p. 230; ibid., p. 239.

24. Edward R. Murrow, Freedom House Award speech, June 28, 1954, quoted in Mark Bernstein and Alex Lubertozzi, *World War II on the Air: Edward R. Murrow and the Broadcasts that Riveted a Nation* (Naperville, Ill., 2003), epigraph.

25. Nicolaus Mills, *Their Last Battle: The Fight for the National World War II Memorial* (New York, 2004), pp. 1–2; Thomas B. Grooms, *World War II Memorial, Washington, D.C.* (Washington, D.C., 2004), p. 110.

26. Grooms, *World War II Memorial*, p. 34.

27. "Friedrich St. Florian Architect," biographical statement on architect's website, http://www.fstflorian.com/Biography.html (accessed January 2007); Mills, *Their Last Battle*, pp. 140–43; Grooms, *World War II Memorial*, p. 23; Thomas Keenan, "The Greatest Veneration: Questions for Friedrich St. Florian," *New York Times Sunday Magazine* (July 1, 2001).

28. "D.C. Memorial for 'Greatest Generation' Opens Monument on Mall," *Boston Globe*, May 28, 2004.

29. Forrest C. Pogue, "Marshall, George C.," in Eric Foner and John A. Garraty, eds., *The Reader's Companion to American History* (Boston, 1991), p. 702.

30. Franklin D. Roosevelt, Transcript of Joint Address to Congress Leading to a Declaration of War Against Japan (1941), http://www.ourdocuments.gov (accessed June 2006).

31. Grooms, *World War II Memorial*, p. 23.

32. Penny Coleman, *Rosie the Riveter: Working Women on the Home Front in World War II* (New York, 1995), p. 40.

33. Yellin, *Our Mothers' War*, p. 51.

34. Ibid., p. 146.

35. "Fun Fact about the United States Mint," http://www.usmint/gov/about_the_mint/fun_facts/index (accessed February 2006).

36. Column for April 24, 1943, in *Eleanor Roosevelt's My Day*, p. 288.

37. Ernie Pyle, column for December 14, 1943, quoted in David Nichols, ed. *Ernie's War: The Best of Ernie Pyle's World War II Dispatches* (New York, 1986), p. 172.

38. Photo caption in Ambrose, *D-Day*, first photo supplement.

39. Ernie Pyle, column for August 28, 1944, quoted in Nichols, *Ernie's War*, p. 353.

40. Garson Kanin, quoted in Terkel, *The "Good War,"* p. 373.

41. Ernie Pyle, column for February 22, 1945, quoted in Nichols, *Ernie's War*, p. 370.

42. "Navy Nerve Center," *Bureau of Naval Personnel Information Bulletin* (September 1944), p. 2.

43. Grooms, *World War II Memorial*, p. 94.

44. Winston Churchill, quoted in Thomas B. Allen, "Victory at Sea," in Brinkley, ed., *The World War II Memorial*, p. 48; Warren Kimball, "Lend-Lease," in I. C. B. Dear, gen. ed., *The Oxford Companion to World War II* (New York, 2001), p. 533.

45. Grooms, *World War II Memorial*, p. 11; William L. Bird Jr. and Harry R. Rubenstein, *Design for Victory: World War II Posters on the American Home Front* (New York, 1998), p. 22.

46. Yellin, *Our Mothers' War*, pp. 167, 216.

47. L. Douglas Keeney, *Buddies: Men. Dogs. And World War II* (Osceola, Wisc., 2001), p. 12.

48. "D-Day," *American Experience* series, PBS, online transcript available at http://www.pbs.org/wgbh/amex/dday/ (accessed February 2006).

49. Ambrose, *D-Day*, p. 46; Dwight D. Eisenhower, quoted in ibid., p. 45.

50. Ernie Pyle, column for August 12, 1944, quoted in Nichols, *Ernie's War*, p. 341.

51. "Battle of the Bulge," *American Experience* series, PBS, transcript available at www.pbs.org/wgbh/amex/bulge (accessed February 2006).

52. Archibald MacLeish speech, December 2, 1941, quoted in Bernstein and Lubertozzi, *World War II on the Air*, p. 118.

53. Grooms, *World War II Memorial*, p. 11.

54. "Amphibious Warfare," in *The Oxford Companion to World War II*, p. 25.

55. Column for September 16, 1943, in *Eleanor Roosevelt's My Day*, pp. 308–9.

56. Kennedy, *Freedom from Fear*, p. 813.

ABOUT THE AUTHOR

Author Michelle Krowl.
Author's collection

Michelle A. Krowl received her Ph.D. in history from the University of California, Berkeley in 1998. Her dissertation examined African American women in Virginia during the Civil War and Reconstruction, and she has also written on women of the Civil War and the reburial of the Confederate dead in the North. With Bradley E. Gernand, she co-authored a history of Quantico, Virginia. While researching this book, Michelle developed an affection for World War II–era aircraft, evident in the 1940s military aviation motif of the Hawaiian shirt she wears above. Dr. Krowl is a research assistant for historian Doris Kearns Goodwin and an adjunct instructor at Northern Virginia Community College.

Dr. Krowl dedicates this book to her father, George L. Krowl, who passed away as the project went into the production stage. George admired the legendary Marine John Basilone, enjoyed WWII movies, and had wanted to produce a line of "Kilroy was here"–inspired gifts, so the dedication of a WWII-related book to him is entirely fitting.